INNATIOUS

INNATIOUS

An innovative tool to strengthen
your emotional IQ and improve the
quality of any relationship

LINDA BUSCEMI, PH.D.

Project
You

ISBN (softcover): 978-1-7353707-0-5
ISBN (MOBI): 978-1-7353707-1-2
ISBN (EPUB): 978-1-7353707-2-9

Front cover design by Melanie Votaw
Interior book design by Eric Myhr

Published by ProjectYou by Doc B LLC
3104 E. Camelback Rd. #520
Phoenix, Arizona, 85016, U.S.A.
projectyoubydocb@gmail.com

First printing edition 2020.

For my spouse, Scarlett Spring.
Her constant encouragement, support, and
undying love through this entire process
have been vital.

Table of Contents

Introduction

A re human beings inherently self-centered? I hold the foundational belief that we are, but bear with me as I explain further. As you will see, this belief includes no judgments.

Through the years, my practice has focused on helping people gain greater self-awareness, leading them to a more in-depth understanding of the true motivations for their actions. As we explored the origin of these motivations, I found that if someone felt they were "accused" of self-centeredness, they immediately became defensive. Thinking of this as a negative attribute equal to selfishness, they set about trying to convince me that they actually weren't self-centered at all. So, I began to say the following to lower their defenses: *"All people are self-centered. The only difference between a four-year-old and a 40-year-old is that the 40-year-old actually knows the world doesn't revolve around them. They know that to get along with others, they have to take the feelings of other people into consideration. Other than that, we all want what we want."* I watched my clients' shoulders drop, one after another, with a great sense of relief.

Self-centeredness doesn't negate caring or empathy for others, but since we can only exist in our own skin, we default to viewing another's experience through the filter of *our own* experience. Therefore, we can put ourselves in someone else's shoes and feel deeply for them, but we will still be connected to our own feelings and experience. We will still be centered within the *self.* This is not a negative thing to be lamented. *It simply is.* In other words, it's natural to want to gratify ourselves, even as we care for others.

I found that when my clients reached this level of self-awareness and understanding, their work with me and their therapy reaped the greatest reward. This insight stimulated the most significant changes in each person.

Believing I was on to something, I continued to explore how to better explain the foundational insight that we, as humans, are instinctively driven to meet our own needs, even as we love and care for others. I set out to create a new word without the stigma of the word "self-centered." I wanted a word that better defines the dynamic I'd observed in my practice, as the definition of self-centered didn't fit what I was trying to express. But such a word doesn't exist, so I created one myself. That's how the term "**Innatious**" was born.

Innatious is defined as *an innate, instinctual desire to please ourselves even in the process of serving others; the premise that our actions, reactions, and behaviors are an innate, often subconscious, and even unconscious[1] desire to fulfill and gratify our*

---

1. Think of the conscious mind as the part of the iceberg that shows above the surface of the water. The subconscious mind is the first part of the iceberg that's hidden under water, while the unconscious mind is the part of the iceberg hidden in the deepest water. Therefore, it's usually easier to access the subconscious mind than the unconscious mind.

inner needs. In simple terms, Innatious is the ability to emotionally identify our needs so that we understand what really drives our actions, beliefs, and emotions.

It's important to note, however, that Innatious is not synonymous with selfishness. Understanding your Innatious intent simply gives you better insight into why you do or feel the way you do.

Is Innatious the same as intention? No. Having an intention, by definition, is conceived, planned, and purposeful. Thus, it is *intended*. It's a direct aim or plan toward something. Innatious intentions, on the other hand, are subconscious or unconscious intentions, which means we aren't consciously aware of them until we make the effort to bring them into consciousness. Because they're outside of our awareness, they can cause us to become "stuck" in our communications and relationships with others. Becoming aware of our subconscious or unconscious Innatious intent or "Innatiousness" gets to the root of the reasons for our actions so that we can evaluate them and make changes to improve our relationships and our life.

Not realizing our Innatiousness leads to an inept attempt to communicate our needs, as well as recognize the needs of others. And, of course, authentic communication is the key to any healthy relationship.

INNATIOUS IN EVERYDAY LIFE

We think of charitable gifts and random acts of kindness as selfless and virtuous actions. I contend that while they are indeed virtuous, they aren't selfless. The result may appear selfless, but, as I said, a key reason why we're giving to charities and performing these virtuous acts is because they give us pleasure and cause us to feel good about ourselves.

It's the feelings of joy and pleasure from charitable giving that provide the Innatious portion of this virtuous act. Giving to others makes us feel good, and since that's the only feeling we can truly experience from the action, it's our Innatious intent. Again, Innatious is not a selfish act. It simply allows us to peel back the layers covering what drives us and recognize that gratifying ourselves also drives our "selfless" behaviors. There's absolutely nothing wrong with the fact that virtuous behaviors are not 100% selfless. I contend that complete selflessness isn't possible, and there's no reason to wish it were.

Another example of Innatious intent in giving to a charity might be the opportunity to clean out our closet and get rid of things. We had a choice to throw the items in the garbage, give them to friends, sell them in a yard sale, or donate them. But donating them fulfills a positive feeling that the other options do not, and that positive feeling is the Innatious intent.

Of course, Innatiousness can also cause us to do things we later regret. Here's an example: Roberta walks into her boss's office to discuss the results of a project she's working on for her company. During the meeting, her boss mistakenly credits her with an aspect of the project that Roberta had nothing to do with. In fact, it was Roberta's friend, Marie, who should receive the accolades. Even though Roberta knows she should correct her boss's mistake, she stays silent and takes the credit. Afterwards, she's wracked with guilt.

What happened here? As she worked on understanding her actions, Roberta came to the conclusion that in failing to correct her boss, her Innatious intent was to feel confident and accomplished. But she was also well aware that what she did was wrong, and this weighed on her, causing her to feel guilty. Now that she knows she has such a need to feel confident and accomplished, she can work on filling that need without resorting to deception.

As you continue reading the pages that follow, you'll find many more examples of how Innatious plays out in your life and how using this concept to increase your self-awareness can significantly improve both your relationship with yourself and your relationships with others.

While you may worry that Innatiousness negates empathy, I've found that it has actually increased my clients' ability to empathize with others. When we think about the Innatiousness of others, we tap into the feelings of the other person and access our deeper empathetic skills.

Many people go through decades of life coaching, counseling, or other self-awareness practices without ever realizing their Innatious intentions. It's a missing piece that's actually the key driver of who and what we are as human beings.

So join me on this exploration of self-awareness, and discover that your humanness is nothing to be ashamed of. By owning up to the feelings that drive you in your life, you'll be able to be more authentic with greater integrity, access your deepest capacity for empathy, and judge the Innatious intentions of others less.

THIS BOOK IS FOR YOU IF ...

- You want to improve communication in your relationships;

- You sometimes act in a way that you regret and wonder why you did it, worried that you might do it again;

- You judge yourself and/or others frequently;

- You hide your true self in relationships with others and worry that the real you will be found out;

- You find it difficult to maintain positive relationships with others; and/or

- You simply want to develop greater self-awareness and more harmonious relationships.

Bottom line: This book is for anyone who wants a deeper understanding of themselves and stronger relationships with others.

Let's start by revisiting Abraham Maslow's Hierarchy of Needs and its relationship to Innatious.

1

Innatious, Needs, and Emotional Intelligence

We are designed to protect ourselves and do whatever we need to do to survive. It's our instinctual nature. When a stove is hot, for example, we instinctively pull our hand away without thinking if we "should" or not.

We react similarly to protect ourselves emotionally. This innate instinct consisting of self-defense mechanisms and automatic thoughts is the emotional foundation of who we are as human beings. And these instincts are at the core of our Innatiousness.

Our Innatious intent is based on what we feel we need. You're probably aware of Abraham Maslow's Hierarchy of Needs pyramid. Although there is some debate on his theory, I believe it provides a solid foundation for understanding our needs as human beings, including a basic sequencing as to how those needs can be fulfilled.

There are five levels to the pyramid. At its base, Maslow believed we must first meet our physiological needs such as breathing, food, shelter, water, and sleep. We're motivated to act, change, and do whatever is necessary to meet these fundamental physiological needs.

Once they are fulfilled, Maslow suggested that we become motivated to fulfill the next level—our safety needs, including a sense of security, our own health and the health of our loved ones, and employment/income.

When the first two levels are satisfied, we're better equipped to focus on the third level, which is the need to feel loved and have a sense of belonging with others. It's certainly more difficult to focus on fulfilling this need when we have no home or food to eat.

The fourth level is esteem, where Maslow focused on our desire for confidence, self-esteem, and respect from others. As you can see, the higher we get on the pyramid, the more attention is paid to the emotional self.

The top level of the pyramid is the desire for self-actualization, where we have the bandwidth to be creative, solve problems, and let go of prejudices. Some people believe we're incapable of achieving this level, but Maslow described it as our potentiality, seeking to become what we didn't know we could become. I believe we can achieve this level but never fully sustain it to the extent that we no longer have to consider the other four levels. In other words, I think there is fluidity between the levels and a continuous effort to reach the top.

The underlying message at this top level is that when we reach Maslow's peak of self-actualization, we supposedly stop thinking of ourselves and become "selfless." I believe the opposite.

To achieve a truer level of self-actualization, it's imperative to examine ourselves and what truly drives our behavior. When we can identify our own genuine drivers, our Innatiousness gives us the capacity for greater empathy and desire for "selfless" acts.

Innatious is an important element to create and maintain healthy relationships. When we don't include it, there's a lack of full transparency, a disingenuous philanthropy, and a denial that separates us from truth, instead causing us to operate in service of the ego.

The main benefit of Maslow's Hierarchy of Needs is that it indicates what we need to work on in our lives and within ourselves to remain more consistently in the top tier, where our self-actualization includes an understanding of our Innatiousness, as well as the Innatiousness of others.

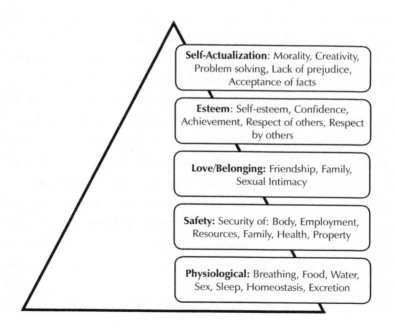

EMOTIONAL INTELLIGENCE

In order to sustain the self-actualization level as much as possible, we need "emotional intelligence" (EI). This concept, developed by psychologist Daniel Goleman, is a specific kind of self-awareness that connects us to our emotions so that we understand our feelings. This EI also increases our ability to empathize with others.

Empathy is the capacity to understand or feel what another person is experiencing from within *their* frame of reference. The more we're in touch with our own emotions and needs, the better we're able to identify the emotions and needs of others.

Innatious and emotional intelligence both promote an awareness of our own motivations and needs, which in turn helps us comprehend the motivations and needs of others. So while Innatious is an understanding of our "self-centeredness," it's also an awareness that actually helps us become more empathetic to others. We're able to comprehend their Innatiousness without judgment, as we realize that we all have Innatious intentions.

Maslow's pyramid and Goleman's EI concept are excellent tools for bringing our needs and Innatious intent into our conscious awareness so that we can be clearer about what we really want and how to obtain and communicate those desires in a healthy way. However, since our true needs, our Innatiousness, can be complex and hidden within the subconscious or unconscious mind, emotional intelligence helps us uncover them. Knowledge of Innatious further helps us dig deep to understand the "why" of our behaviors. We can then use that knowledge to alter destructive behaviors and make decisions that are in true service of our needs.

Here's an example of how Innatious intent comes up in complicated life situations. Diane is a junior in college who has just finished finals for her semester. She's supposed to leave in the morning for a much-needed spring break vacation.

Then, she gets a call that her grandmother has been taken to the hospital with a heart problem. Diane's family reports that her grandmother is fine, but the doctors want her to stay in the hospital overnight for monitoring. Of course, Diane wants to be there, but she feels conflicted because her well-deserved vacation is hanging in the balance. Should she go on spring break, or should she cancel and go home to see her grandmother?

This internal struggle can be maddening, but understanding her Innatious intent will help her sort through it. Of course, Diane's first thoughts and feelings are of love, concern, and care for her grandmother. But underneath those feelings are frustration, sadness, and even anger, which are all in conflict with her feelings of concern. So what is her Innatious intent in this situation? She doesn't want to feel guilty for not being there during a family emergency.

While knowing her Innatious intent may not change her decision, it should prevent resentment about it later. She will be able to own her choice without blaming anyone else, knowing that she made it from a conscious place after considering all aspects of the situation, including her inner thoughts and emotions.

Many of us are fearful, in denial, or unwilling to admit the Innatiousness of the situations in our lives. We become confused when we experience conflicting emotions, but it's common and perfectly normal to experience love, concern, guilt, and even anger simultaneously. There's an internal battle between the need to please ourselves and the desire to please others, while avoiding the negative feelings associated with whatever choices we make.

But the more we develop our EI, the better able we are to process all of these emotions quickly and sort through them to understand our Innatiousness and the Innatiousness of others. It's important, however, to specifically look for our Innatious intent, as traditional self-awareness leaves out this important part of our unconscious material. Someone might be self-aware enough to know they're upset if they can't go on their vacation, for example, but they might still feel resentful without the knowledge of Innatious. Only with this expanded awareness can we take full ownership of our decisions without projecting responsibility onto anyone else. This ability gives us the maturity to enhance and preserve our relationships with others.

INNATIOUS IN RELATIONSHIPS

We can, in fact, use our awareness of our Innatiousness to improve our communication skills. Here's an example: John and Maria had been together for two years, and they were becoming serious enough to discuss marriage. As part of that discussion, they agreed they didn't want to spend the Christmas holidays apart. They would put their relationship first, celebrating Christmas with John's family the first year and Maria's family the following year, alternating like this during subsequent years.

When their second Christmas together drew near, however, John began to negotiate for traveling to visit his family, even though they'd visited them for the holidays the year before. Maria reminded him of their agreement, but he told her it was going to be very hard for him. It was the first time in his life that he would be away from his family on Christmas, and he had no idea how it was going to affect him until the holiday season came around. As the weeks got closer, he became noticeably distraught.

When he spoke with his family, they couldn't understand why he wouldn't travel to see them. He tried to explain the agreement with Maria, but his parents and siblings weren't happy. As John explained his dilemma to Maria, she remained calm but firm that she wasn't going to travel to be with his family. She would keep their agreement and spend Christmas with her own family. This led to long discussions about trust and what they wanted for their lives.

Yet, John's anguish grew stronger, and Maria began to question his ability to keep promises. It also led her to wonder if she would ever come first or if he'd always put his family before her, even after they were married.

One evening, John was on the phone with his brother and mother, and it was clear that the pressure from his family was escalating. When he hung up the phone, he told Maria that while he didn't want to break their agreement or lose her trust, he was truly struggling and couldn't understand why the situation made him so emotional.

Maria was upset, but she used her emotional intelligence to pause and think about John's possible Innatious intent from an empathetic standpoint, looking at the situation objectively and taking her emotions out of the equation. She knew he was experiencing deeper feelings than the ones on the surface. Certainly, he wanted to spend the holidays with his family, but there was something more at stake for him that was intensifying his feelings. Then, it came to her. "Are you grieving?" she asked him.

John looked up at her, and a sense of relief came over him. She was right. He was grieving a 45-year ritual with his family. This awareness led him to come to another Innatious intent below the surface: He was also feeling guilty that his excitement about his new life with Maria might hurt his family tradition. His need, his Innatiousness, was to avoid the grief and guilt about this change in his life, how it impacted his relationship with his family, and how he could communicate harmoniously with them. If John didn't understand his Innatiousness in this situation, he might hide his life from his family and hold back when communicating with them.

Identifying John's Innatious intentions allowed both of them to discuss the situation with deeper emotional intelligence. The knowledge immediately eased the intensity of John's feelings, and they worked together to develop a plan that fulfilled them equally without throwing blame back and forth. The solution involved John identifying what he loved about Christmas and which memories were essential to him to capture. They decided each would travel to their respective families *before* Christmas for a period of time and then fly back Christmas Eve night so that they could wake up together on Christmas morning. This allowed them to honor their agreement while also giving John time to reframe a new ritual with his family.

In hindsight, this situation may seem trivial or even simple to navigate. But in my private counseling practice, I've seen this scenario spiral out of control, often creating long-term trust issues that eventually cause relationships to fracture. Because they sought the Innatiousness in their circumstance, John and

Maria were able to take accountability for their
without blaming the other. Because Maria und€
tious and practiced empathy, as opposed to taking ... _
personally, they had a productive and healthier outcome that
strengthened, rather than weakened, their relationship.

In a healthy relationship, we have a lot to manage—empathy,
self-preservation, defense mechanisms, automatic thoughts,
our ability to problem solve and cope, and past experiences and
programming. Understanding our needs, developing deeper EI,
and identifying our Innatious intent, as well as that of others,
gives us a better chance of satisfying or resolving the issues we
face. When we don't do this, it often leads to resentment, blame,
and projecting negative feelings onto others.

INNATIOUS DRIVERS

In the example of John and Maria, they came to the conclusion
that John's Innatious intent was to avoid feeling grief and guilt.
Another way of putting it is that avoiding grief and guilt were
Innatious *needs* for John, and those needs became *drivers* of his
feelings and behaviors. These were situational for him, however,
as we all have fundamental Innatious needs or drivers in our
lives. For most of us in the western world, these Innatious drivers fall into the third and fourth levels of Maslow's pyramid.
We want to feel loved, respected, confident, and accomplished.
Our behaviors are then *driven*, usually on a subconscious or
unconscious level, by these needs/Innatious drivers.

When we develop a better understanding of our fundamental Innatious drivers, we can avoid a great deal of conflict in
our lives. The only way we can change something is to become

aware of what actually needs to change in order to improve our circumstances. If we blame someone else or misinterpret our own feelings and behaviors based on a low emotional intelligence quotient (emotional IQ), we may inadvertently spin our wheels or cause harm to ourselves and others.

Remember the story in the Introduction in which Roberta's behavior was driven by her need to feel confident and accomplished (fourth level on Maslow's pyramid)? Since she was unaware of her Innatious drivers, she ended up doing something dishonest that caused her a great deal of pain and guilt. She might also have a fundamental Innatious driver to avoid pain and guilt, but because of her need to feel confident and accomplished in the moment during her meeting with her boss, she inadvertently threw herself into a situation that caused exactly the opposite, while also causing her pain and guilt.

With greater self-awareness and EI, Roberta could have caught herself in that moment, noticing that she was tempted to allow her boss to mistakenly credit her for someone else's work. Then, she might have had the strength to stop herself from making that mistake, understanding that her Innatious drivers and behaviors were in play to her detriment. This awareness could have led her to work on creating better situations for herself to feel confident and accomplished or perhaps even soften the intensity of those Innatious drivers through therapy.

Let's look at one more example that comes up in a lot of our lives. Think about when you love someone, and they love you. It feels like the best relationship you've ever had. You flourish as individuals and as a couple. You're able to communicate how much you love each other and why. You may say things like,

"You're beautiful, funny, smart, and confident." And all of those descriptive words are true! But where is the Innatiousness?

At the end of the day, even though all of these characteristics and reasons for loving someone are true, it's how that person makes *you feel* that sustains the relationship. There's a country music song written by Victoria Shaw and Chuck Cannon that was recorded many years ago by John Michael Montgomery called "I Love the Way You Love Me." The song explains Innatiousness in love relationships well.

What does the other person do for you? Challenge you? Enable you to feel smarter, empowered, special, safe, secure, and/or desired? You may still think of this as selfish, but it isn't. It's simply the truth of human nature.

Let's say a man falls in love with a beautiful woman. Having her in his life makes him feel desirable and special, and he relishes the envy of his friends when he shows up with her gracing his arm. The problem is that they don't have anything in common. He's so blinded by his Innatious drivers to feel desirable and special that he doesn't notice their lack of common interests. The two of them marry, but over time, the fact that they don't want the same things wears on the relationship.

With the emotional intelligence to become aware of these Innatious drivers, he might have been able to see that the relationship was doomed to fail. He could have seen the superficiality of their connection and opted instead to fill the needs for feeling desirable and special with a partner who could appreciate him on a deeper level and vice versa.

What about your own needs and Innatious drivers and behaviors? Let's try an exercise to help you begin to become more aware of these aspects of your subconscious and unconscious.

HIERARCHY OF NEEDS EXERCISE

This exercise will allow you to rate yourself on Maslow's Hierarchy of Needs scale. This will help you determine where you want to focus additional attention to be fully present in your life.

Answer each question on a scale from 1–5, with "1" meaning "no problem" and "5" meaning a huge stressor for you.

1. **How much stress surrounds your *Physiological* needs (having food and water, sleep, living accommodations, etc.)?** *When we have an illness or trouble finding where our next meal is going to come from, there is a barrier for us to be reflective or fully focus on other higher level needs.*

    ☐ 1   ☐ 2   ☐ 3   ☐ 4   ☐ 5

2. **What is your level of *Safety* (focusing on the security of your environment, employment, resources, health, etc.)?** *When we don't feel secure/safe, if we're unemployed, or don't have other safety needs met, it may cause us to tap into our primal instinct of survival. The desire to self-reflect and increase relations with others is then lower on the need scale.*

    ☐ 1   ☐ 2   ☐ 3   ☐ 4   ☐ 5

3. **Do you feel a sense of *Belongingness* (focusing on love, friendship, intimacy, family, etc.)?** *Feeling like you belong is an important aspect of your emotional and mental health. We all want to feel loved and accepted, and when we don't, it can affect other levels on the Hierarchy of Needs.*

    ☐ 1   ☐ 2   ☐ 3   ☐ 4   ☐ 5

4. Where is your level of *Esteem* (focusing on your confidence, self-esteem, achievements, obtaining respect, etc.)? *People like to have a purpose. When we don't, it can hinder our confidence and cause confusion regarding why we're here.*

   ☐ **1**   ☐ **2**   ☐ **3**   ☐ **4**   ☐ **5**

5. Where do you rate your level of *Self-actualization* at this point in your life (focusing on your morality, creativity, problem-solving, etc.)? *This level of need is very fluid depending on the fulfillment of our other needs. This need provides the ability to be more authentic and introspective for continued self-evolution.*

   ☐ **1**   ☐ **2**   ☐ **3**   ☐ **4**   ☐ **5**

What did you discover about your needs? Are you surprised by the results? Are you in a position to worry about basic needs, or are your needs primarily focused on the emotions of the top three levels?

EXPLORE YOUR INNATIOUS DRIVERS

1. Knowing what you now do about your needs on Maslow's pyramid, what do you think are your fundamental Innatious drivers?

2. Which needs in your life are being fulfilled, and which are not?

3. Think about your primary relationship. What do you want most from this relationship? Do you want to feel loved

and respected? Do you want to feel needed and/or special? What's most important to you? These are your drivers or motivators. Write down two to five drivers.

4. Think about your work/purpose. What do you want most here? Do you want to feel respected, important, confident, accomplished, and/or needed? Write down two to five drivers.

5. Think about your friendships. Do you want to feel liked, respected, and needed? Do you want to receive attention from others? Write down two to five drivers.

6. If you struggle to come up with answers for these, think about situations in your life in which you felt unfulfilled, frustrated, or angry. Which of your needs or Innatious drivers were not being filled? In what situations have you been *most* satisfied and fulfilled? Which of your needs or Innatious drivers were taken care of in these relationships or circumstances? Asking yourself these questions will help you determine what drivers are primary in your life. For example, my main Innatious drivers are to feel needed, receive attention from others, and feel that others believe I'm worthy.

7. Next, ask yourself about your main Innatious drivers with regard to avoiding negative experiences. In my case, my main Innatious drivers are to avoid conflict, guilt, and feelings of unworthiness. In life situations in which you've felt frustrated or angry, what were you trying to avoid feeling? These are your main negative Innatious drivers. Write down two to five drivers.

8. What happens when you don't get these main needs filled in your life? What behaviors do you resort to? For example, if you don't receive attention from others, perhaps you feel unworthy. This may cause you to withdraw and feel depressed, or it could cause you to try too hard to get attention from others. Maybe you even pick fights to get attention.

9. When you make a mistake, do you feel like a failure, which causes you to lose self-esteem? What do you do to try to then fill this need for self-esteem? Do you feel defeated and put yourself down, or do you strive harder next time? Do you find yourself putting others down in order to lift yourself up? These are your Innatious behaviors. Write down two to five of these behaviors you've noticed. (Try not to judge yourself for any insights you may find disturbing. If you discover something you dislike about yourself, take heart that this new awareness will allow you to begin to alter your behaviors and improve the quality of your relationships.)

10. For each of the behaviors you noted, how have these behaviors affected your relationships (either personal or business) with others?

11. Reflect on the answers you've given to these questions. How do you believe your Innatious drivers and behaviors have affected your life, both positively and negatively?

12. Reflect on ways you might begin to notice the Innatious drivers and behaviors that are negatively affecting your life and change the way you react.

2

The LAR Scale

We all want to be happy. It's what most of us say is our ultimate goal in life. But what is happiness? When I ask people to define it, they usually pause. It isn't an easy question to answer. It becomes even more complex when we try to assess our happiness level within a relationship. How do we even know when we're happy?

Jim is certain he'll be happy when he finally becomes a partner in his law firm. Sharon hates her apartment, so if she could only save enough for a house, she'd finally be happy. For Rhonda, it's about the love relationship that has remained elusive in her life so far. And for Timothy, it's about having enough money to travel, never worry about paying his bills, and maybe even buy a yacht.

The world is filled with people who believe happiness is based on finances or the attainment of goals like these. But when they obtain that house, that promotion, that relationship, that yacht

... then what? Does the happiness fade? Must they find another item to want in order to activate the carrot of happiness again?

On some level, we know these things will only provide a short-lived feeling of joy, but the question remains: Do they make us truly happy? And if they don't, what *does* create long-term happiness?

I find that as human beings, our desires tend to be similar. But there are three areas that I believe make up the core of our internal happiness: *Love, Acceptance, and Respect.* We all want these three things. They are all part of our fundamental Innatious intentions in relationships. If we don't receive these in a relationship, we will likely feel less fulfilled, and the connection will probably be unhealthy.

Those three words represent a form of control, power, confidence, and a feeling of inspiration to move forward. But how do we attain them? First, it's good to assess where we are in our relationships right now.

THE LAR SCALE

To assess our levels of Love, Acceptance, and Respect, I have created what I call the "LAR Scale." It can help you quickly assess your relationships and determine where you are on this spectrum of relationship happiness. It isn't scientific; it's simply a practical guide built from my years of observing people that quantifies satisfaction level in relationships. You simply score from one to ten (with ten as the highest/best) your degree of Love, Acceptance, and Respect for the other person. Then, you score the level of Love, Acceptance, and Respect that you believe the other person feels for you.

I invite you to try this exercise at home, and if possible, have the other party in the relationship try it as well. Obviously, you need to have open communication so that any discrepancies and misalignments between your scales can be used to discuss ways to improve and enhance your relationship rather than lead to an argument. If there's conflict between you, however, it might be better to take the assessment and discuss it in the presence of a therapist.

When used productively, the LAR Scale allows us to understand each other and determine where some of our needs may not be met, including the realization that unintentionally, we may not be fulfilling the other person's needs. Many times, we don't even realize how we have impacted the people in our lives. This is a great way to get a clearer understanding.

Please bear in mind that you might define these words differently from your partner, and those definitions could account for the differences in your assessments. Learning these differences can be illuminating in your relationship and help you communicate with each other more clearly.

For example, loving someone can be an all-encompassing feeling of safety and companionship, a sense of trust in the other person, and/or appreciating the way that person treats you. In defining Love, there is an underlying Innatious intention with regard to the *action* of love. How are you fulfilled by the other person's love for you? This is important because lack of fulfillment is the biggest barrier when a relationship begins to be challenged. Sometimes, people justify or defend their change of heart by blaming the other person.

Obviously, relationships can be tricky, and people come in and out of our lives. One overarching reason for this is that as we age, change, and evolve, so do our viewpoints, perceptions, and Innatiousness. So the people who fit with who we are and what we want also change. When that happens, the two parties probably didn't grow and change together, managing and evolving their Love as their lives changed.

For example, Jason and Barry had been together for ten years when Barry met someone else named Eric. Barry found that he felt more loved by Eric than he had ever felt with Jason. Eric hung on every word that Barry said and listened intently, which allowed for intense, fascinating conversations. Jason, on the other hand, having a high-pressured career, tended to have a lot of anxiety about all the things he had to do. This caused him to be distracted regularly so that he didn't listen well. Jason didn't mean to be a bad listener, of course, but as a result, Eric filled needs for Barry that Barry didn't even know he had. It caused the bar for fulfillment to be lifted higher than it had been during his last ten years with Jason. So his love for Jason began to wane, as he felt like he was falling in love with Eric instead.

Whether or not Jason and Barry can salvage their relationship depends on a lot of factors, but if they were to talk openly with one another about their Innatiousness and work with the LAR Scale, they might be able to fill each other's needs better. Ideally, through communication and awareness, they would have caught this issue before it took a stranger to make them aware of the lack of fulfillment in their relationship.

What about Acceptance? How does that play into our happiness and Innatiousness? Being able to accept ourselves is an important aspect of happiness. But even if we get to a place of accepting ourselves, it's painful when others don't accept us.

Having acceptance from others can validate and gratify us, especially when we receive acceptance from those we love.

It's an essential need in relationships to feel we're accepted for who we are, how we look, our diverse thoughts, and even for the others we may love. When we aren't accepted, or the other person appears condescending or negative about us, the relationship will naturally erode and experience a divide. A simple example is if your loved one doesn't accept your sense of humor, rolling their eyes at something you find funny. Or perhaps you have different values that your partner can't accept. It's important to note that acceptance isn't about having to agree on everything. Instead, it's about accepting and appreciating your differences without ridicule or negativity.

Here's another example: When Chloe and Scott got married thirty years ago, they were in their early twenties and didn't think much about compatibility. At the time, they both loved going to rock concerts and playing tennis, and that seemed to be enough. As they got older, however, neither of them liked going to rock concerts or playing tennis anymore. Throughout the relationship, they were busy raising their children and building their careers, so they never stopped to think that they needed to cultivate their relationship as well. They just assumed it would take care of itself because they did love each other.

But suddenly, when their last child went off to college, they realized they had little in common anymore and barely even knew each other. It isn't that they didn't still love each other to some degree, but that love had waned due to years of inadvertent neglect. Without children at home, Scott found himself wanting to retire early and travel, but this would mean a substantial reduction in their income. He was burned out from decades of working hard to build his career and increase the family's income so that they could enjoy the fruits of his labor. Chloe contributed to the family income as well, but losing Scott's salary and digging into their retirement fund early made her feel fearful about their future. She had no desire to travel and felt that Scott was being irresponsible and immature. The change in their income would force her to make sacrifices she was unwilling to make. She couldn't accept this new Scott, and he couldn't accept that she wouldn't go along with what he felt he needed. He had a long bucket list and felt he had only a short time to begin checking off the places he wanted to visit.

The Innatious intentions of both Chloe and Scott to be accepted in their relationship were in jeopardy, putting a damper on their happiness with each other. If they could come to an understanding through transparent and vulnerable communication, perhaps with the help of a therapist or coach, they might be able to reach an agreement that would allow them to accept one another again. Otherwise, their relationship might no longer fit the people they had become.

It's important, of course, to understand Chloe's and Scott's Innatiousness. Bringing to awareness why each feels the need to stay home or the need to travel is imperative to move the relationship into compromise. Scott's Innatious desire to retire and travel may be coming from an avoidance of fear of dying early as his father did and not having an opportunity to enjoy retirement. Chloe's Innatious intent to not travel could be at least partially due to a desire to spend time with her grandchildren. Once we understand our own Innatious intentions and those of our partner, accepting the true root of everyone's decisions and desires, we're much more willing to work together toward a solution.

The final core value of the LAR scale is Respect, which is about having an appreciation for the other person's qualities, skills, abilities, and achievements. It's about respecting who the other person is, as well as what they have to offer.

Here's an example of how loss of respect can undermine a relationship: Peter and Melissa had been together for five years. Peter had just been promoted and was under a lot of pressure at work. When he made a big mistake on a project, he lied to his superiors about it and did everything he could to cover it up. He even ended up getting a couple of his colleagues in trouble in the process. He was constantly on edge that he would be found out.

While he continued to try to cover his tracks at the office, he decompressed about it at night to Melissa. He was completely transparent with her, telling her exactly what he did. Peter assumed Melissa would understand his decision given the situation, pressure, and new dynamics he was under to prove himself.

But unbeknownst to Peter, Melissa was extremely disappointed in him. She had always thought of him as someone with high integrity, and suddenly, she saw a side of him she'd never seen before. She saw a deceptive and fearful person that she didn't recognize anymore. She told herself that if she were in his shoes, she would have owned up to her mistake and faced the consequences. She couldn't imagine allowing colleagues to take the blame for something she had done. She hadn't yet told Peter how she felt, but she wasn't sure she would ever be able to see him in the same way. At the same time, she worried that she was being too judgmental and unloving about the failings of her partner. She was glad he felt he could talk to her. If he had shared this dark secret, it would have likely hurt their relationship. She struggled with how to reconcile the person she thought Peter was with this uncharacteristic action of deceit.

When they tried the LAR Scale, Peter was floored by the low rating he got for Respect from Melissa, but immediately realized that his behavior at work was the culprit. While he felt tremendously hurt and even a bit defensive, the score allowed the two of them to begin to talk openly about how they felt. It wasn't easy for Melissa to disclose—or for Peter to hear—but they continued to work together to try to come up with a solution.

Peter expressed his remorse about what he did and agreed to work on developing his integrity so that he would act more responsibly in the future. He talked about how his parents punished him extensively whenever he made a mistake as a child. This knowledge allowed Melissa to have more compassion for Peter. She felt comfortable that he acknowledged his misgiving and would work on this issue within himself.

The LAR Scale is just one more tool that helps us unearth our Innatious intentions and become more transparent in relationships. The more truthful we are, the greater the level of intimacy we achieve, and the better chance we have of addressing our true issues. This is how we salvage the relationships we want to keep. The awareness it provides also allows us to leave relationships that no longer serve us, without blaming others or leaving behind lifelong resentments.

Recognizing where you are on the LAR Scale is important not just for your relationships, but also the relationship to yourself. When others rate you high on the LAR scale, but you don't feel that way about yourself, it can help you see yourself in a better light.

Dana and Alex, for example, were pleasantly surprised by the results of their LAR Scale assessment. Alex had struggled with low self-esteem for years and had no idea that his wife would rate him so highly on all three elements of the scale. For a long time, he had put himself down internally for any mistakes he made, and he assumed Dana's respect for him was diminished by every failing. He was shocked and delighted to be proven wrong. Dana actually was impressed by how Alex rose above any negative feedback and the doors that were closed to him. He persevered and moved forward to get what he wanted in spite of the obstacles. She actually aspired to be more like him.

Dana felt similarly to Alex, however. She had always felt inferior to him and many others, but when she discovered how much her husband loved, accepted, and respected her, it allowed her to recognize some of the qualities that Alex appreciated about her. The result of the exercise for this couple was that it brought them greater awareness of the depth of their Love, Acceptance, and Respect for each other. It also helped them to see that they had been too hard on themselves in terms of their own self-worth. They realized they hadn't given themselves credit for how well they persevered through the tough times. The ultimate outcome was that their relationship was rejuvenated, and their happiness levels increased.

The truth is that the crux of happiness lies within fulfilling our needs while our natural instincts as social and sexual beings and our need for our relationships help foster our happiness. Regardless of our level of comfort in social situations, we human beings are social creatures. Whether we call ourselves an introvert or an extrovert, relationships with others are important. It isn't good for us to stay in our own heads all the time. It's productive to share what we're thinking and process it with others, especially if those thoughts are negative or become self-detrimental. When we don't share our thoughts, we assume many things because we only get perspective from our own very biased source within. Obviously, as we saw in the case of Dana and Alex, this can happen even within a close relationship simply because we don't usually communicate so transparently with one another.

TRIGGERS

Emotional triggers can muddy up LAR Scale scores. What are triggers? They are emotional reactions to issues that we are particularly sensitive about. Remember Peter and Melissa? When Peter made the mistake at work, he was "triggered" by it because his parents had punished him for making mistakes when he was a child. This trigger caused him to try to hide the mistake rather than take responsibility for it.

Think back to a time when you realized you overreacted to something someone else said or did. That overreaction is due to being triggered by something from your past. These issues from our past are usually locked away in our subconscious or unconscious mind, so only when we bring them into our conscious awareness can we begin to calm our overreactions. For example, let's say your mother always acted as though you weren't capable of taking care of yourself. It hurt you and caused you to become vehemently independent in order to prove her wrong. Then, one day, your friend says something that you interpret as meaning she doesn't believe you can take care of yourself, and you become very upset. Your friend may not even think you aren't capable of caring for yourself, so she may be perplexed by your reaction. This is what I mean by a trigger.

When we allow these triggers to remain outside of our conscious awareness, they can cause us to interpret the words and actions of others incorrectly. These triggers are responsible for the fracturing of many a relationship, and they can certainly come into play when scoring ourselves and our partner's feelings on the LAR Scale.

One of the advantages of the Scale is that it can bring this unconscious material to light so that we have the opportunity to see our triggers for what they are and begin to lessen their power.

TRY THE LAR SCALE

The real benefit to working with the LAR Scale is the ability to honestly assess your most valued relationships in the categories of Love, Acceptance, and Respect. Wherever there is a gap, you have a beginning discussion point. The goal in your discussions is to be curious as you strive to understand what it would take to get to the highest level of ten. If you and someone else are both taking the assessment, make a pact not to judge the other person for their score numbers. You may find yourself feeling shocked, but try to stay with that feeling rather than move into anger, defensiveness, and blame. This exercise will help you determine your Innatiousness, which will likely decrease any negative feelings that come up. However, if you feel you can't avoid an argument, work with a therapist as you disclose your scores.

It's also important to remember to integrate your Innatiousness in your discussion. What you want for yourself—what you want to feel and experience in the relationship—is important to share with the other person.

When your relationships are on the higher end of the LAR Scale, it's an indication that you have reached a space of vulnerability with each other and a better understanding of how to communicate. You have found a healthy, loving way to challenge each other to grow. The ability to share your struggles with your loved ones from a safe space of no judgment is the very essence of happiness. Most people fail to see the importance of this degree of intimacy because they fear it so much, but finding the root cause of such struggles and having Innatious as part of your communication style are key components for a healthy relationship.

Working to reach the top of the LAR Scale will help you find this utopia within yourself and in your relationships. When you use the LAR Scale to quantify at least one relationship, you can sit down and think about what the numbers truly mean for you and the relationship.

As you embark on the exercise with someone else, set rules. If the other person becomes defensive, respectfully bring this out into the open. Remember: The score is how the other person is feeling, and feelings aren't wrong. They simply are what they are. Feelings may be misguided based on interpretation, but the key to the LAR Scale is to begin talking about why you are thinking differently and then, explore how you can move toward being on the same page.

Here are some other tips for how to work with the LAR Scale harmoniously:

1. Remember that the number is a point of discussion, not a measure or "value" of the relationship. Please forego judgment of the numbers you assign to each relationship. Just be honest.

2. Don't use "tit for tat" or "one-up" scenarios. This exercise isn't about measuring what you do or don't do for each other or for bringing up past grievances. LAR is about learning what your loved one feels and discovering the Innatiousness of both parties. It's how you can learn and support that person for the betterment of your relationship.

3. Be sure to use "I" statements rather than blaming "you" statements. For example, avoid saying something like, "You make me feel unlovable." No matter how it may seem, it

isn't the other person who "made" you feel that way. Take responsibility for the fact that the other person's actions, reactions, or comments have simply triggered something within you from the past that caused you to feel unlovable. You may respectfully point out that their tone of voice, expression, or posture felt demeaning to you, but you must be responsible for how you then react to the trigger. You can only control your reaction to someone else's behavior. You can let them know how you feel and ask them to be aware of their communication delivery and that it triggers you. But if they can't or won't change, it's up to you to neutralize the trigger within yourself. By doing so, you're empowered to no longer base your feelings about yourself on what someone else does—even if that person is your spouse.

4. Commit to changes based on the LAR exercise that will help you explore Innatious intentions, create a healthier relationship, and better fulfill each other's needs.

THE LAR SCALE EXERCISE

For the relationship you want to assess, ask yourself:

- From 1 to 10, with 10 as the highest, how much do I feel I Love this person?

- From 1 to 10, with 10 as the highest, how much do I feel I Accept this person?

- From 1 to 10, with 10 as the highest, how much do I feel I Respect this person?

- From 1 to 10, with 10 as the highest, how much do I feel this person Loves me?

- From 1 to 10, with 10 as the highest, how much do I feel this person Accepts me?

- From 1 to 10, with 10 as the highest, how much do I feel this person Respects me?

Then, ideally, have the other person answer the same questions to see how aligned your answers are with each other.

As you discuss the numbers, you may begin to think Innatiously about why the two of you have these scores. Next, you might think of how your level of happiness can increase as you increase your LAR Scale scores. Would you like the level of respect you receive to go from a five to a six? Do you think you could bring it to a ten? What may be preventing you from obtaining that higher score?

3

You Teach People How to Treat You

Kelly and Justin had been dating for just over a year. From the beginning, Justin often changed plans without asking or communicating the change to Kelly until the last minute. He would show up at her house to pick her up and say, "Hey, we're going to meet Sam and Susan instead of going to the movie." This happened on average a couple of times per month, to which Kelly would respond, "Oh, okay, that's fine" or "Sounds good."

She never gave any indication to Justin that she was upset or irritated. But internally, Kelly became increasingly frustrated. As her tolerance grew thin, the couple began having small arguments. Still, Kelly never explained to Justin why she was mad. She would just snap at him for little things that, if she was honest, didn't bother her like his frequent changing of plans.

If you put yourself in Kelly's shoes, do you believe she has a right to be irritated that Justin doesn't include her in the changes of their plans? One viewpoint is that it's wrong for him to change what they're going to do without consulting her. You might even say that Justin should know better. But what if he doesn't know better? Kelly didn't express to him that this bothered her, so she didn't "teach" Justin that she wanted to be consulted about what they were going to do.

This type of scenario happens to many couples. The frustration comes out, but no one communicates transparently what's truly bothering them. In some cases, the frustrated party may not even understand what they're frustrated about, but they begin to have negative feelings toward the other person.

Through therapy, Kelly realized that early in their relationship, she was so infatuated and in love with Justin that she overlooked anything he did. Her Innatious drivers were to continue feeling the excitement, lust, and connection to him that she felt at the start. This Innatious intention drove her to devalue her own feelings and not say anything. Yet, after months of this behavior, her Innatiousness shifted. She was no longer fulfilled or gratified solely by the excitement and lust. Instead, she began to feel unappreciated and disrespected. The combination of the shift in her Innatious intent and Justin's lack of knowledge about the shift led to miscommunication between them. It's natural to grow and evolve in our relationships, but if we don't stay aware of our changing needs and then communicate them, relationships can quickly go south.

Now, let's talk about Justin's part in this scenario. You may ask: If Justin is a good guy, why would he take advantage of Kelly and not consider her in his decisions? The first point to consider is if his behavior is malicious. Did he purposely disregard Kelly's thoughts and feelings? Could it be that he thought Kelly preferred for him to be the plan-maker and that she was fine with spontaneity and last-minute adjustments? Justin may have thought he was impressing Kelly by taking charge and being spontaneous. You see, while we can speculate about another person's Innatious intent, we never know for sure unless we ask them probing questions. And of course, we don't even know our own Innatious intent without digging deeper within ourselves to find out. Justin might want to consider his lack of awareness and why his Innatiousness was being fulfilled by someone who would do whatever he said without expressing her own opinion.

The point of this story is: *We teach people how to treat us.* Due to her Innatious desires, Kelly wasn't honest with herself about her feelings. There was some benefit to her overlooking Justin's behavior. It allowed her to avoid going deeper. Early on, her Innatiousness was to keep the gratification she felt from being on the arm of this handsome and charismatic man. It may be uncomfortable to admit, but it was these primal Innatious desires that were driving her decisions. By keeping her true feelings to herself, Kelly inadvertently taught Justin that it was fine for him to treat her this way.

If you apply this to your own life, you might think, "No way do I teach people how to treat me!" or "I certainly don't teach people to be mean to me!" Well, the truth is that yes, you do play a role in how a person treats you, both positively and negatively. No one is "doing" anything to you. Rather, you have allowed a pattern of treatment from others. (Bear in mind that in this context, I'm not talking about a situation where someone is physically abused and unable to escape the perpetrator.)

If you find yourself in a situation in which someone is repeatedly treating you in a way you dislike, you must ask yourself how you're creating that pattern by not making your feelings known. And if you've made your feelings known, and the other person continues to ignore those feelings, why are you still in the relationship? If you choose to be there for your own Innatious reasons, you have to take responsibility for that choice. Sometimes, we do decide to accept someone's inability or unwillingness to honor our boundaries. It's your choice which boundaries are deal-breakers and which ones allow for compromise, but if you compromise repeatedly, it's bound to be to your detriment.

How many times have you gotten frustrated because you felt you couldn't say "no" to a friend or colleague? Does it happen frequently or infrequently? How often do you compromise your desires and, therefore, your boundaries? The level of frequency is an important metric because compromise is a natural component in all intimate relationships. Without a healthy give and take, lasting relationships are virtually impossible. But if there's a consistent imbalance where one person compromises much more than the other person, the relationship will struggle to survive. It's important to recognize if you're allowing someone to cross your boundaries often.

When people tell me that they resent another person, my first question is: Why have you allowed them to cross your boundaries? My second question is: What are you getting from it emotionally, (i.e., what's your Innatious intent)?

It's unnatural to subject ourselves to discomfort, so exploring the Innatiousness of the relationship is important. What are we getting out of allowing someone to cross our boundaries? The Innatious intent could be to avoid rocking the boat because we fear saying anything will cause the other person to leave us. We might be staying in a relationship for feelings of security, self-worth, or fear of being on our own or alone with our kids. That's our choice, of course, but it helps to come to terms with the true reasons for our choices. We can then gain perspective about the compromises we made for the relationship, and rather than direct our dissatisfaction at the other person, we can perhaps come to a place of greater acceptance.

Our Innatious intent is to either receive a positive benefit or avoid something negative. In this situation, we are avoiding the negative feeling of abandonment. While this is an understandable fear, allowing our boundaries to be violated repeatedly is not only dysfunctional, but a recipe for disaster. Few relationships can stay together under these circumstances, and if they do, I question the satisfaction of either party. For the period in which we do permit violations, we have not only allowed the other person to treat us poorly, but we've treated ourselves poorly. That causes a lot of damage in both the relationship and in our psyche. This relationship pattern, unfortunately, will likely continue until our Innatiousness is identified and worked through.

When you're aware of your Innatiousness, you naturally have higher emotional intelligence, and you understand why you choose the relationships you do. That's key to maintaining successful relationships that can endure life's changes.

You must understand your behavior, decide if you like it, and then adjust it or react differently based on how you want to act toward others, as well as how you want them to perceive you and act toward you. As you continue to work on yourself, building and maintaining your confidence and self-worth, especially as you age, it's vital to communicate and work with your loved ones to ensure both people are fulfilled in the relationship.

When you become upset because of how you're being treated, you must ask yourself if you've taught this person to treat you a certain way based on your past responses. Have you enabled this treatment, and if you decide that you're no longer going to tolerate the behaviors, what then? Once you "change the rules" of how you wish to be treated, should you inform the other person of the rule change? Yes. And I'll address that in a moment.

SETTING BOUNDARIES IN A HEALTHY WAY

Setting boundaries with the people in our lives is important for our sense of self-worth. It's the only way the other person can know what is and what is not acceptable to us. We make a big mistake when we assume other people will just "know" what we're okay with and what we're not okay with.

So it's a great idea early on in relationships to be direct about our boundaries. If we do that, we can often prevent boundary violations—the kinds of violations that can trigger us and cause us to feel distrustful of the other person. As soon as our trust is weakened, the relationship is on shaky ground. When we strive to be direct, we immediately set the relationship on a stronger foundation.

First, it's important to know yourself well and what you're comfortable tolerating and compromising in your relationships. If you've had trouble setting boundaries, it's helpful to understand why you allowed the behavior. Again, what is your Innatious intent in allowing someone to cross your boundary? What are you avoiding?

If you wish to change a dynamic in a relationship, you must first change how you respond and react to it. When you are ready to express your need for a boundary, be emotionally ready, cautious not to over-explain, and be gentle without blaming the other person. After all, you're changing the "rules" in the relationship, and the other person might be surprised and resistant at first. Don't place blame. Instead, use "I" statements rather than "you" statements. Avoid saying something like, "You always choose the restaurant and never even ask me where I want to go." Say something more like this: "I've recently come to realize that I always let you choose the restaurants we visit even though I don't always like them. In the future, I plan to express my opinion, and I'd appreciate if we could discuss it openly so that we find a restaurant where we both want to eat." Remember that you taught this person to treat you a certain way, so clear and caring communication is key.

Another practical example is regarding shared tasks in the home. Amelia always leaves the dinner table without placing her dishes in the sink. For years, Rafael has swallowed his irritation about this and cleared the table himself. If Rafael abruptly begins to react negatively to Amelia's behavior, it will probably cause issues between them. A better approach would be for him to pitch this at a time when there are no distractions. Both Amelia and Rafael need to be in a calm state for the conversation to go well.

Rafael could begin by taking responsibility for his part: "Amelia, I'd like to talk to you about something and apologize for not bringing it up sooner. I've cleared the table and done the dishes for years, but the truth is that it has bothered me. It was my responsibility to say something, and I didn't. But I'd really appreciate it if from now on if you would help me out by placing your dishes in the sink after we're finished eating. Can we agree to that?"

Make sure, of course, that you allow the other person to speak, and listen without interrupting. Avoid judging their feelings as best you can. Remember that our initial feelings are sometimes only a surface layer that may come from a defensive standpoint. So if you're calm and ask follow-up questions, it helps to sift out the Innatiousness.

The most important step is to stay calm. It's also important to plan for success by having the discussion when you have sufficient time away from TV and other interruptions.

We have to compromise and strike a balance in all healthy relationships, and when we want to be treated differently, we have to stay consistent. This means that once you communicate a boundary to someone, you have to uphold it. You can't allow them to violate it again. And you also can't count on someone to uphold the boundary unless you remind them. Remember that you're asking the rules to be changed, and the other person's behavior may be habitual. So try to stay calm and gently remind them if they cross your boundary after you have expressed it to them.

DIGGING DEEPER INTO INNATIOUS INTENT

When boundary conflicts come up in relationships, it's usually because our individual Innatious drivers are in conflict with one another, or at least they seem to be in conflict. Most of the time, people don't mean to cross our boundaries. They're simply tied up in their own Innatiousness like Justin was with Kelly or Amelia was with Rafael.

It's important to go deeper when we try to figure out our Innatiousness, however, because what may at first appear like a selfish act may be about something else entirely.

For example, Carl and Abigail were in conflict because Abigail felt that Carl was lazy and taking advantage of her. He liked to be a couch potato on the weekends and especially during football season. He often had his friends over to watch a game, not realizing that the shopping and preparations on Abigail's part were extensive, as she supplied food and drinks to everyone. Carl seemed to just expect Abigail to wait on them all.

When they explored their Innatious drivers, Abigail believed that Carl's Innatiousness was simply to be lazy and not exert himself. But when they dug deeper, they discovered that for Carl, it was about feeling loved and cared for. When Abigail did these things for him, he felt her love for him, and he needed that. His mother had expressed her love in this way. She never actually told him she loved him, but she took care of him and never asked him to do much for himself. Even after he moved out of the house, all he had to do was take his laundry to his mom, and she would do it for him.

Unknowingly, Carl had chosen another woman (Abigail) who didn't express her love verbally. In this case, however, Abigail became increasingly unwilling to take care of Carl in the way his mother had done. After all, he was a grown man. Yet, she hadn't "taught" him to treat her differently until the situation escalated to the point that they finally sat down and talked about it.

It took some work to dig deep enough to find the true Innatious driver behind Carl's actions, and Abigail began to discover her own, which was to feel that she, too, was cared for. When it came down to it, they both had similar Innatious drivers. She showed her love by cooking and even enjoyed the accolades she received from Carl's friends when she cooked for them. It gave her confidence and a sense of pride. But over time, the expectation that she would cook for his friends became excessive, as it was virtually every weekend during football season.

Once they came to this awareness and talked about it, they laughed. Carl was more than willing to step up and also do things for Abigail so that she wouldn't be expected to do all of the work when his friends came over. Even though it would be an adjustment for him, he didn't want Abigail to feel put upon. He wanted her to be happy and to feel his love for her. They also agreed to verbally express their feelings of love for each other more often. At first, they felt awkward about it, but it didn't take long before they enjoyed the verbal expressions, as well as exchanging a more balanced expression of love in their actions toward each other.

This process may initially be scary, as it takes both people to be vulnerable, but once you have gone through the exercise of discovering your Innatiousness, it becomes much easier.

CODEPENDENCY AND INNATIOUS

Codependency is behavior in which we habitually put the needs of others ahead of our own. We typically think of codependency as those who enable loved ones with an addiction, but it's much more widespread than that.

Those who are codependent struggle to see any boundaries between themselves and others. They become emotionally enmeshed with others and sometimes feel that the people they love can't survive without their help. It can be hard at first to even determine what they want separate from others. You may have had an experience in which you asked someone their opinion, only to have them immediately tell you their spouse's opinion rather than their own. This is sometimes an indication of codependency.

In some respects, codependency comes from a deep feeling of love and empathy, but as you know, there is another layer. The Innatious intent may be to feel safe in the relationship. Therefore, if they take care of the other person, all will be well. But these needs go to extremes, often not allowing the other person involved to take responsibility for their own behavior. This shows us that sometimes, our Innatious intentions aren't always in our best interest but are based on fears and childhood dysfunctional patterns that we need to bring into our conscious awareness and heal. In other words, there are underlying Innatious drivers that can allow us to *truly* get what we need rather than what we *believe* we need due to the fears that cause our codependent behaviors.

In the process of codependency, we tend to lack healthy boundaries and allow other people to treat us in a way that compromises us. One example involves Tim and Jake, who have been dating for 15 months. Tim is more gregarious and giving, while Jake is more detailed, attentive, and passive. Both are successful in their careers, but Tim makes more money and comes from an impoverished childhood, so he tends to spend freely to help others. Jake is also from a low socioeconomic background and makes decent money, but he never has any extra money at the end of month. There's an assumption in their relationship that Tim will pay for all of their extracurricular activities, such as dinner, movies, and weekend excursions. Jake has even called Tim to pay for an Uber ride to work for him when Tim was out of town on business. Jake is very close to his family, and there always seems to be drama in the family dynamics. He sometimes pouts and is prone to emotional outbursts. He brings drama into their relationship, expecting Tim to "fix" things, especially when it comes to money. While Tim complains about Jake, he tries to be understanding and often goes ahead and solves the problem. Bottom line: Tim likes feeling needed. This is an ideal backdrop to breed codependency and unhealthy behaviors.

Another example is the person who overcommits, trying to be all things to all people. This person's Innatious intent is to feel self-worth through being helpful and useful, but again, that intent has become extreme. This usually happens when the person's self-worth is low, and they feel they must prove that worth through numerous 'selfless' acts. They believe that saying "no" to someone would reduce their self-worth, so they don't dare say "no." But they say "no" to their own well-being when they refuse to ever say "no" to others.

People who never say "no" usually end up resenting others and blaming them for their busy schedule. Many times, this person turns into a martyr: "I never have time for myself, but I love to help." The Innatious interpretation in this situation is that they're afraid they won't be loved if they say "no" to someone. They're afraid to be abandoned, and doing for others assuages their anxiety. But it's their own responsibility to choose what they can realistically do and what they truly *want* to do rather than what others expect of them. And it would be healthier to deal directly with the fears of abandonment, as well as cultivate self-esteem without the need to over-give.

What about someone who always goes along with what their partner wants to do, only to feel resentful later? For example, Benjamin was brought up to believe that being a gentleman meant always doing what the lady wanted to do. So whenever he and his girlfriend made plans, he asked her what restaurant she wanted to visit and what movie she wanted to see. He even let her choose their vacation locations without his input. As a result, he frequently ate food he hated, saw movies he didn't care to see, and even spent lots of money on vacations that he just pretended to enjoy. Over time, he started to resent that he never got to do what he'd like to do, but he still believed this was the way a relationship must be.

Meanwhile, his girlfriend, Jessica, was oblivious to his feelings because he never told her. When she suggested a very expensive vacation destination that would compromise Benjamin's financial plans, he began to see her as a user—a money-hungry person who only cared for herself. So he finally blew up, and all the frustrations he'd bottled up came out in an explosion that sent Jessica out the door in a state of confusion. The result was the end of the relationship without either of them fully understanding what happened. They were both doomed to go through the same issues in their next relationship unless they became more self-aware and discovered the importance of knowing their Innatious drivers.

Benjamin's Innatious driver in this situation was to be a good man—a gentleman who was worthy of Jessica's love. But he first needed to question his childhood belief that being gentlemanly meant the denial of all of his own needs. If he could develop a more balanced and realistic definition of a gentleman, he could fulfill that Innatious intent without also becoming codependent and perhaps avoid the demise of the relationship.

He also needed to understand that another Innatious intent was to avoid losing the approval of his parents. He believed their approval was contingent upon his ability to be a "gentleman" based on their definition, even though their approval may or may not have anything to do with what he thought.

While our behavior is often learned, the emotion behind the behavior is also usually learned, even if that emotion doesn't really make sense. Once we're aware of this unconscious material, we can begin to change. In Benjamin's case, he was playing out a ritual that wasn't truly his own and that he didn't consciously believe in. But because he wasn't aware of this disconnect between his childhood beliefs and his adult beliefs, he blamed Jessica for the problem.

As for Jessica, she needed to examine her Innatious drivers in choosing a partner who denied his own needs and never tried to compromise. It could be that she felt deprived in a past relationship and was trying to compensate by making sure her partner put her first. This dynamic validated for her that she was special and made her feel like a "queen." It would be helpful for her to explore why she needed that kind of validation from her partner and how that need had affected who she was attracted to.

It might be hard for Benjamin to voice his own wants in his next relationship. It's a new behavior for him, and he'll probably worry that it will put the relationship in jeopardy. But his revelation of his Innatious intent is to not only be a gentleman based on his redefinition of the word, but to also take good care of himself and get his own needs met. Change like this takes time, but the true Innatious awareness provides the best ammunition to work toward a more satisfying relationship.

People who are codependent like Benjamin usually struggle with guilt when they begin to set boundaries and allow their own needs to be met. They have no doubt been conditioned from childhood to be "selfless" and try to make sure everyone is happy before they make themselves happy. This, of course, is unnatural because Innatious is simply human nature. It isn't our responsibility to take care of everyone else's needs to the detriment or abandonment of our own.

Let's explore the boundaries or lack thereof in your own life.

BOUNDARY WORKSHEET

Answer the questions below as honestly as you can.

1. Do you communicate your thoughts, feelings, opinions, needs, and desires to others? If not, why not? What holds you back when you want to share?

2. When someone asks you what you're thinking, how often do you tell them the truth?

3. Do you allow yourself to become overwhelmed with commitments to others and then get upset with them because of it?

4. Do you find it difficult to say "no" when others ask you for help?

5. What drives you to do something you don't want to do?

6. Do you hold back from others because you don't want them to think you're "weird"?

7. Do you fear if you set boundaries that you will lose people you love?

8. Think of one time in your life when you set a boundary with someone else. What was it like, and how did it feel? Did the other person become upset with you? If you had handled it differently, do you think it would have gone better?

9. Think of one time in your life when you didn't set a boundary with someone to your detriment. What was the ultimate outcome?

10. Do you remember the steps to engage another in a dialogue regarding behavior change?

The next time you want to set a boundary with someone, plan what you will say.

4

The People We Choose

Ralph had a series of friendships that ended badly. Every time he connected with another friend he seemed to find himself in an argument that caused the relationship to fracture. He couldn't figure out why it kept happening to him with his friends and, sometimes, even colleagues.

Even the nature of the arguments was similar from one friend to the next. After the last fallout with his friend/colleague, Ralph's girlfriend finally convinced him to see a therapist about the situation. He came to understand that he had a pattern of choosing friends who were spontaneous, fun, and exciting to be around. Ralph, on the other hand, tended to be quiet and a little bit shy.

When he explored his Innatious drivers, he realized that he enjoyed being with these men because they helped to bring him out of his shell. He admired their gregariousness and ability to talk to anyone. He liked the way he felt when he was around them, and he wanted to be like them. A part of him hoped their personalities would rub off on him, but at minimum, he was living vicariously through them by virtue of being in their presence. This is not uncommon. as many of us pick friends with characteristics we want in ourselves.

The problem was that these same friends were also irresponsible and sometimes even unkind to others. So, eventually, the relationship would end because Ralph couldn't tolerate their tendency to treat others carelessly, including blowing off plans or even expecting him to always be the designated driver or pay their way at bars and clubs. Why is Ralph picking friends who are bullies and exploitative of others, when there are people with similar characteristics who aren't jerks?

Through therapy, Ralph became aware that these friends were triggering him, as he experienced bullying as a child. He desired to be in the "cool" crowd even if he paid for drinks and was the designated driver. But as time went on, his past was triggered, and he couldn't remain silent about how his friends treated others. This boomerang behavior highlighted his Innatious intent to feel accepted and part of a spontaneous and adventurous group. By understanding his drivers, he could begin working on his self-esteem and begin to cultivate true friendships that were more balanced, (i.e., both spontaneous *and* respectful that the relationship should be a two-way street).

Most people tend to attract the same kinds of relationships, whether personal or business, and that tendency is largely a result of their Innatiousness. When these patterns create relationships that are out of balance, they cause conflict, confusion, and sometimes pain.

All healthy relationships—whether with family, friends, colleagues, or lovers—need to have a balance where both parties are fulfilled, while each person also agrees to make compromises. Most relationships ebb and flow with the scale tipped from time to time, but the overall scale should always balance out throughout the span of the relationship. If the scale is consistently tipped unevenly to one side, the imbalance will cause a lack of fulfillment and a feeling of discomfort for at least one of the two people.

Sometimes when the scale is uneven, it's because the relationship is failing to challenge one or both parties to evolve and grow into their potential, or perhaps it's stifling them from becoming who they want to be. The bottom line is that when a relationship scale is chronically uneven, the relationship isn't likely to be healthy.

But why do we stay in relationships that are out of balance?

THE INNATIOUSNESS OF THE RELATIONSHIPS WE CHOOSE

Attraction, connection, and infatuation are all drivers in choosing a romantic partner. Whether the attraction is physical, emotional, mental, spiritual, or a combination of these, we're sometimes attracted to people whether they're good for us or not. When you think about the type of person you're attracted to, what are the characteristics that come to mind? Strength, confidence, adventurousness, caring? Do you tend to choose someone who is a "yes" person—passive and never a challenge? Or do you tend to choose someone who argues with you constantly?

The greater question is *why* you're interested in these characteristics. Perhaps someone would choose a "yes" person because they have a fear of being wrong. That way, they don't have to feel challenged in their insecurities.

Have you ever been in a relationship with someone who had most all the characteristics you believed you wanted, yet you still weren't happy? Have you ever had a happy relationship with someone who didn't have so many of the characteristics you said you wanted?

We choose the people in our lives because they fulfill something for us. We respond to how they make us *feel,* whether that feeling is positive or negative. Sometimes, we choose someone who makes us feel terrible about ourselves, but we do it because that terrible feeling is familiar. This person may treat us like one or both of our parents, and the familiarity is oddly fulfilling for us because we haven't resolved the negative experiences from childhood. Unconsciously, we don't feel we deserve anything better.

Obviously, understanding our Innatiousness in relationships will be the greatest eye-opener as to why we choose certain people or remain in specific relationships. Sometimes, it's as simple as, "I like his caring nature because it makes me feel secure" or "I like that she challenges me because I grew up in a home where there was a lot of good-natured arguing. So, that kind of challenge translates into love for me."

Let's begin with great relationships. Subjectively, I will define "great" as a well-balanced, satisfying connection between two people who have LAR scale ratings of 8 or higher. In seeking love, acceptance, and respect, we usually choose to spend most of our time around people who are like us—people we can relate to and who can relate to us.

Feeling satisfied in a relationship allows us to feel a sense of freedom to be who we are and say what we want to say without worrying that we'll be judged. People in great relationships have patience and acceptance for each other. They allow the other person to be less than perfect. They appreciate the characteristics of their partner, even if those characteristics bug them some of the time. They don't try to change the person. They simply communicate their needs so that the two of them can work together for the fulfillment of each other.

This is where compromise comes into play. Decisions made in a relationship, from where to eat to where to live, must be made collectively. We must compromise for the better of the unit of one, not as an individual. This isn't always easy since we sometimes don't align on major decisions. And remember, our instinctual desire is to gratify our own Innatious needs. Empathy and an increase in our emotional intelligence are what lead us to consider compromising, helping, and gratifying others as we also seek to gratify ourselves.

Healthy, great relationships also provide a supportive platform for both parties to grow and better themselves. Good partners help each other to discover and overcome their insecurities and negative beliefs.

When two people share a life in an intimate relationship, it's important to consider the two people as one unit, while also keeping the fulfillment of each individual's desires in mind. If this sounds complicated, it's because it is. And it's exactly why relationships can be difficult to sustain. Satisfying everyone isn't always possible, as our needs can sometimes conflict too much.

For a relationship to be considered "great," "challenging," or something in between, there are a number of variables, but your rating on the LAR scale is a good place to start.

Now, let's consider relationships that tend to be "challenging." In this case, LAR scale scores are usually 6 or under. Our LAR needs are at the very core of what fills our Innatiousness. Therefore, when our scores are low, we aren't fulfilled or gratified in the relationship.

If that's the case, however, why do so many of us stay in these relationships that score so low on the LAR scale and fail to fulfill us? Sometimes, our Innatious intent is negative, but unconsciously, we see it as a positive.

Bonnie and Ray, for example, had been together for three years. Bonnie had a habit of putting Ray down and rolling her eyes when he tried to help her with virtually anything. He felt like he couldn't do anything right in her eyes, no matter how hard he tried. "Why did you buy avocados that are so ripe, Ray? These are going to go bad before we can eat them." Those were the kinds of things she said to him on a regular basis.

There's no question that it was wearing on him, and Ray complained to one of his friends about the way Bonnie treated him. If he were to use the LAR scale, we would see that Ray didn't particularly feel loved, accepted, or respected by Bonnie. Nevertheless, he never said anything to her about his feelings, nor did he consider leaving the relationship.

So, if Ray's LAR scores were so low, why would he ever stay with Bonnie?

It took some digging for Ray to discover his Innatious drivers in this situation, but eventually, he realized that his need to be with someone rather than alone was stronger than his need to be loved, accepted, or respected. In other words, his insecurities about being alone and the intensity of that fear drove him to stay in an unhealthy relationship. Unconsciously, he was convinced that being alone would be much worse than the verbal abuse he received from Bonnie. He was also unsure and insecure about his ability to attract anyone kinder. He concluded that he could do no better than Bonnie. As a result of these fears and beliefs, his LAR needs were put on the back burner, leaving him unfulfilled and believing he wasn't capable of creating anything different in his life.

Through therapy, Ray was able to recognize that his beliefs were false. First of all, he and his therapist explored whether being alone would *truly* be worse than enduring someone else's constant scorn. Second, he was questioned as to whether he was truly incapable of attracting another woman into his life and asked what evidence supported this belief. That was a more tenacious belief for him, but he continued to remind himself that he had a lot to offer in a relationship.

Unfortunately, Bonnie was unwilling to see a therapist with Ray, so it wasn't long after his new awareness that he made the decision to leave the relationship. While he could only speculate as to Bonnie's Innatious drivers, he wondered if her Innatious intent was to feel superior. She had once told him that her mother had put her down a lot, so he thought perhaps she was projecting her internal dialogue onto him. Instead of putting herself down in her head, it gave her some relief to put him down instead. So, perhaps her unconscious Innatious intention was to release the relentless, critical voice of her mother in her head by making it about Ray. To heal this, Bonnie would have to agree to work on bringing this voice into consciousness. Only then could she notice the negativity and counteract it on a daily basis until it was no longer so relentless. But her Innatiousness in refusing to get help was the fear of finding out something negative about herself. Her Innatious intent was to continue to think of herself in the right and preserve a false sense of self-esteem based on denial. We have probably all made this unhealthy choice at some point in our lives.

If you find yourself in a relationship with a low LAR score for you, it takes honesty with yourself to uncover the Innatious drivers that keep the relationship at such a low rating. And it takes real work with both individuals to raise their respective LAR scores and hopefully save the relationship. Of course, if your partner is unwilling to do that work, you have the choice to leave.

Bonnie wasn't satisfied in her relationship with Ray either, but she was in denial about her Innatious intention for staying with him and even why she was attracted to him in the first place. She rushed to defend herself and blame the situation fully on Ray, who "couldn't do anything right" in her view. It would have been painful to become aware that she was projecting her internal criticism onto Ray. She was too afraid to learn this, so she remained in denial, probably destined to attract another man like Ray, whose Innatiousness would "match" her own in a negative way—someone who would let her continue the pattern. She was unaware that the short-term pain of learning the truth about her Innatiousness would truly be much less painful than the long-term pain of maintaining her dysfunctional pattern. After all, that pattern prevented her from creating a loving and fulfilling relationship.

Ray had also been in denial at first about his true Innatious intentions, but because he was willing to bring them into consciousness, he was able to heal. It was only due to his efforts that he had the opportunity to create the healthy, gratifying relationship he'd always wanted.

When we become defensive like Bonnie, it's an indication that we may be in denial about our true Innatiousness, especially if we jump to blame someone else. In the beginning, Ray blamed Bonnie for his plight. After all, she was the one who was putting him down. But as I said in Chapter 3, we teach people how to treat us. Because of Ray's own unconscious Innatious drivers, he allowed Bonnie to continue to treat him poorly, and he had to take responsibility for that. Once he was aware of the concept of Innatious and accepted his part in the dysfunction of their relationship, Ray wished Bonnie would be willing to do the work he'd done. He felt new compassion for her and wanted her to be happy. But it was work she alone had to be willing to do.

Defensiveness is a particularly destructive force in relationships that causes emotional distance, lack of connection, and imbalance. It's usually a telltale sign that something needs to be brought into awareness.

THE VALLEYS OF RELATIONSHIPS

Sometimes, of course, intimate relationships become stagnant. There are good times, challenging times, and, well ... just time. Given the frequency of the stagnation stage in long-term relationships, the key is how to move forward through these valleys and get back to the peak of happiness and contentment.

Most people call the first year of a love relationship the "honeymoon" period. This occurs because we are "in love" or infatuated with feeling. We also usually feel loved, accepted, and respected. We put our best foot forward to please our mate. We may even over-compromise to ensure their happiness, feeling as though we are securing ours at the same time, when we're actually denying our own needs. As time moves on and we become more comfortable in the relationship, our Innatious intentions begin to shift. The need to feel secure in the relationship decreases, while the need to fulfill our own needs increases. It's within this shift that even a great relationship can begin to stagnate or become challenged.

Since we're products of our experiences and daily internal evolution, the culmination of 365 days per year can bring big changes in our perceptions. These perception adjustments can be about any number of things, including ourselves as individuals, relationships in general, our culture and society, our environment, and much more. When our perceptions shift, our Innatiousness may also shift.

How do these changes affect our relationships? First, are we communicating our newfound perceptions with our mate? If not, why not? If we are, do we discuss how the new perception affects us and our view of the relationship? I often say to people that if you are thinking the same way at age 45 as you did when you were 40, something's wrong! I'm exaggerating and being facetious, of course, but only slightly because we *should* be growing and changing. And it's a lot to expect us to grow and change in exactly the same way.

It helps, however, to contemplate how our perceptions are changing us. This can give us insight into how our Innatious needs are also changing and how to better fulfill them. But it's also important to keep our mate apprised of these adjustments so that we can continue to be on the same page within our relationship. When we talk about these changes as they're happening, the differences are incremental. When we *don't* talk about these changes, the differences will be much more dramatic over time. Suddenly, our partner, who has been completely in the dark about how we're evolving internally, sees us as a completely different person. It's much more difficult to sustain a relationship when that happens.

A classic example is the woman who allowed her husband to make all of her decisions and handle all of the money in the relationship. In the beginning, her Innatiousness was to feel secure and cared for because she didn't have the confidence to make decisions and handle finances. This is a key reason she chose him. Another Innatious driver for her was to be who her husband wanted—someone who was dependent upon him so that he could be the hero. This helped her to feel loved, accepted, and respected. But it also robbed her of her authenticity and independence.

Over time, she developed greater self-confidence and met other women role models who were independent and self-sustaining. As she grew older and discovered more of who she was underneath the desire to please her husband, her Innatious intent was as much to love, accept, and respect herself as to receive those things from her partner. Gradually, she became more aware of her own desires—her healthy Innatious needs—and realized she couldn't be herself within the relationship. When she finally told her husband she wanted a divorce, it was a shock to him because she had never talked with him about the changes that were taking place inside her. If she had communicated what she was learning about herself, they could have discussed it and perhaps worked on a new normal for them as a couple.

Even subtle changes can eventually become dramatic if we don't bring them into awareness and share them with our partner. Maintaining that kind of awareness, of course, requires mindfulness and high emotional intelligence. But it's well worth cultivating those skills. While it may seem like a lot of work, life is actually much easier when we develop the ability to stay aware of what's happening inside of us and communicate it to others when necessary. We save ourselves a lot of internal conflict, as well as conflicts with others. We discover early when a relationship is no longer serving our Innatiousness so that we can try to save the relationship or decide to leave it and move on without wasting time staying in a situation that doesn't satisfy us.

Whether we remain in a relationship or choose to leave it, our Innatiousness is an important guide that helps us make sure we're satisfied with the relationships we choose to keep. And with this awareness, we make our choices from a conscious place rather than from the unconscious fears and beliefs that we carry with us from our childhoods.

We are also able to make better choices when we enter into new relationships. What is our Innatiousness in choosing a particular person as a lover, friend, or colleague, and is that Innatious intention healthy? Will it serve us and help us reach high LAR scores in this relationship?

Of course, there are no perfect people or perfect relationships. But the goal is to "fit" with one another and have a relationship that is healthy and satisfying.

Relationships have a very broad spectrum from great to challenging and everything in between, from our friends, lovers, and family to our acquaintances and colleagues. We must think about what each relationship provides us and brings out in us.

THE PEOPLE WE CHOOSE WORKSHEET

Answer these questions to the best of your ability:

1. What qualities and characteristics are attractive to you in love relationships, as well as friendships and business associations? For example, do the people in your life typically go along with your decisions without challenging you or discussing their own desires? If your gut reaction is to answer "no" to this question, dig deeper and think about it carefully to make sure that's the honest answer.

2. Think about the relationships you value in your life. Do you treat your loved ones differently than people in your other relationships? Are there different "rules" or expectations based on the type of relationship? Are the ratings on the LAR scale different? If so, why? How is your Innatiousness being fulfilled by the characteristics of each other person?

3. If you're in any unhealthy relationships, why do you stay? What are you getting from this relationship, both positively and negatively? Be as honest with yourself about your Innatious drivers as you can.

4. If you uncover negative Innatious drivers, what do you think you can do differently to make a change in your life? Can you work on healing certain fears or beliefs that prevent you from allowing yourself to fully receive your LAR needs in the relationship? If so, what fears and beliefs do you need to work toward healing?

5

Our Perceptions and Defenses

We all perceive things differently based on our experiences, cultures, rituals, religions, beliefs, and more. With those different perceptions, how do we live in a world of six billion people and get along? Of course, at times, we don't. But when we do, I believe it's through understanding that our experiences from birth have a great deal of influence on our thoughts and perceptions. And we all have varying experiences and ways to fulfill our needs.

Each day and each moment, we build upon our existing experiences and perceptions, and we interpret a situation based on our Innatious need in that moment. We're usually unaware of these developments, as they happen in the subconscious and unconscious parts of our mind. Our brains are always working, and it's this unconscious autopilot that carries us through life's ups and downs. Autopilot can be very self-protective—an unconscious defense mechanism that makes conscious change difficult, but certainly not impossible.

How do we gain insight as to why we think as we do? In the musical, "South Pacific," there's a song called "You've Got to Be Carefully Taught" about how we aren't born with prejudices against others—we learn them. The same is true about prejudices and judgments against ourselves. So we must become cognizant of the influences from our past and the beliefs we hold in our unconscious as a result of those influences. It can be surprising to discover that we've based our decisions and behaviors on certain beliefs that were set in our unconscious when we were children. We didn't have the capacity then to question these beliefs, and many of them were due to the inaccurate assumptions of our childhood perceptions. Only when we bring these beliefs into consciousness can we question their accuracy and make a new, more conscious and adult decision about what to believe.

For example, you might have grown up believing that you aren't intelligent. In spite of the fact that you've advanced in your company to top executive status, this belief about your intelligence remains in your unconscious. The drivers of your Innatiousness are to prevent anyone from finding out that you aren't smart. This desire to avoid embarrassment causes you to overcompensate by working harder than necessary, putting in long hours, and even avoiding vacations. This causes problems with your family because they want more of your time and attention.

If you bring into your awareness the understanding of where this belief originated and weigh the evidence to support the belief, you may realize that only an intelligent person could have been as successful in their career. Beliefs like this can be tenacious, however, so it isn't always as simple as saying, "I'll no longer believe I'm unintelligent." You may find that you have to work a bit at changing this belief despite the evidence to the contrary.

As another example, it's well-known and documented that discrimination is taught and modeled. A person doesn't grow up to believe that women are inferior or that homosexuality is wrong. It's human interpretation that drives negativity against other races, genders, ethnicities, religions, and cultures. We're all human and imperfect. The million-dollar question is why can't we be accepting and tolerant of each other and our differences?

Again, beliefs like these can be very tenacious and are usually borne of fear. It's only when we question the rationality of the fear that we can let go of negative beliefs.

DEFENSE MECHANISMS

There are two main emotional reasons for the Innatiousness of intolerance. First, let's discuss two unconsciously automatic self-protection methods that humans use to guard their Innatiousness. The first is the defense or coping mechanism. In short, defense mechanisms are unconscious strategies used to protect us from experiencing anxiety or thoughts we deem to be unacceptable. When we believe we aren't accepted by someone else, an autopilot defense mechanism is triggered to protect us from this negative feeling.

There are many types of defense mechanisms that you'll read about later in the chapter. One of the most common is compartmentalization, which is an effort to separate one part of ourselves from the awareness of the other part. For example, a homicide detective might completely separate his work life from his family life. In order to get through the horrors of what he witnesses in his job, it's best to compartmentalize it so that he doesn't bring it home where he's safe and loved.

A second type of defense mechanism is displacement. This is when we displace our feelings and impulses onto a more acceptable or less threatening target. An example of this is when a boss yells at his employees even though he's actually angry with his own boss.

Denial is another common defense mechanism that happens when we refuse to accept reality because it feels too threatening. A spouse might refuse to admit her husband is suffering from dementia, for example, and simply attribute his forgetfulness to being tired.

The defense mechanism of projection is when we unconsciously shift unacceptable thoughts and feelings onto another person. An example of this might be when a husband has an affair and then accuses his wife of having one.

Another common defense mechanism is passive aggression. This is when we mask or disguise our feelings of displeasure toward another person. If we become upset that chores aren't finished after asking three times, for example, we might insist we aren't upset rather than express our disappointment directly. Then, the anger will come out in snide remarks or irritability.

It's important to understand what defense mechanisms are and which ones we tend to use in life, although most of us have used all of them at some point. Once you have an idea of the defense mechanism you're using, the next step is to determine the anxiety or unacceptable thought you're trying to avoid. Then, you can identify your Innatious intent and begin to prevent the use of these defenses.

AUTOMATIC THOUGHTS

The second self-protection method consists of automatic thoughts. These thoughts stem from the beliefs we have about ourselves. Those beliefs are formed based on feelings from a situation or event, or perhaps they're borrowed from our parents or others who said something to us about ourselves. A simple, "What's wrong with you?" from a parent when we're young can create a belief in our unconscious mind that stays with us for a lifetime as an automatic thought.

Then, that same thought that something is "wrong with us" can be triggered by a number of experiences in adulthood—the fear of asking someone out because we're certain they won't say "yes" since something is wrong with us. Or perhaps we respond defensively when our boss points out a mistake we've made. We don't want to think there's something wrong with us, yet deep down, we believe there is. So if we think someone else is implying it by pointing out a mistake, that automatic thought is triggered. Our Innatious intent in that situation is to avoid the pain of that automatic thought, so the thought leads to a defense mechanism.

Here are a few common automatic thoughts:

Overgeneralization, such as when a one-time event or situation is now seen as a constant rule. For example: "I didn't get the job I wanted. I'm never going to advance." Or: "She broke up with me. I'll always be alone."

Mind Reading occurs when we make assumptions about other people's thoughts without having facts to support our assumptions. For example: "He didn't call after our date.

Obviously, he doesn't like me." Or: "I didn't get asked any follow-up questions, so I think the interviewer thought I was stupid."

Personalizing is when we think something has to do with us when it really doesn't. For example: "My boss is in a bad mood. It must have been something I did." Or: "She's being quiet. I think she's angry with me."

Emotional Reasoning is when we misinterpret feelings as facts. For example, if we feel like a failure, we then believe we *are* a failure. If we feel ugly, we then believe we're truly ugly.

Negative Filtering is when we only concentrate on the negative things and ignore anything positive. This is a symptom of perfectionism. For example, if you're unable to answer one question during a presentation, you deem the entire presentation to be a failure. Or if you get a glowing review at work, you focus solely on the suggestion that you improve your communication skills.

To change our automatic thoughts, we have to first become aware of them. Only then can we begin to catch them in the moment and replace them with a better thought. We can also, in the moment, stop ourselves from being triggered and overreacting to a situation in a way that may cause relationship issues at work or in our personal life.

When my clients identify a negative automatic thought/belief about themselves, I ask them, "What evidence do you have to support this thought as fact?" Rarely can they state anything rational that indicates the thought is objectively true.

For example, Tracy had suffered numerous breakups and was convinced she would *never* have a successful relationship. When asked how she knows this as fact, she recounted all of her past experiences. But Tracy needs to realize that if she learns and evolves, her past doesn't have to predict her future. Since she absolutely can't predict what will happen tomorrow or the next day, there's no way for her to know as fact that she'll never have a successful relationship.

Plus, with each relationship, she has learned more about herself, as well as her likes and dislikes, making her more likely to choose well the next time. And she has many successful relationships with friends, family members, and colleagues.

Similarly, Bruce was sure his boss's bad mood was the result of a big mistake Bruce had made the previous week. He couldn't be convinced otherwise, even though there was no way he could know this for a fact. This assumption was an automatic thought for Bruce that likely came from the times his father got upset with him for getting a B on a test rather than an A. Later, Bruce had similar experiences with a couple of bosses who seemed to fly off the handle over the slightest mistake.

A few days later, though, Bruce's current boss called him and said, "I'm so sorry to bother you with this, Bruce, but my mother has taken very ill. I've been terribly worried about her for two weeks, and now, it appears she may not make it. I'm going to have to fly out first thing in the morning, and you're the only person I trust to take the reins of the new project. Can I count on you to do that?"

Bruce learned from this that his past experiences didn't necessarily predict his fortune in the future.

AUTOMATIC THOUGHTS AND INNATIOUSNESS

Automatic thoughts are part of our Innatious needs. Remember that Innatious means we have an instinctual desire to please ourselves even as we serve others. Our actions, reactions, and behaviors are an innate, often subconscious and even unconscious, desire to fulfill and gratify our inner needs. Our automatic thoughts fulfill our inner desire that the world revolves around us.

Think about the thoughts of a four-year-old versus a 40-year-old. I believe the only difference between them is that the four-year-old believes the world revolves around them, while the 40-year-old *wants* the world to revolve around them but realizes it doesn't. Therefore, the 40-year-old must take others into consideration in order to have healthy relationships. Herein lies the very essence of Innatious. Everything we do is to fulfill ourselves, both positively and negatively, including the avoidance of conflict. We human beings like to feel in control even if the control isn't favorable to us.

Would it surprise you to learn that believing you aren't good enough is a form of control? Yes, it's a negative form, but it's control nonetheless. We find comfort in believing we know the "truth" or have a "clear thought," even if we're mistaken about the clarity or true nature of that belief/thought. In an odd way, believing we know the truth about our own insufficiencies eases anxiety and gives us the illusion of direction and control. We want our thoughts, beliefs, and emotions to be in sync, so we will alter our thoughts and beliefs to agree with our emotions, even if those beliefs and thoughts are inaccurate. It's no wonder that our automatic thoughts can be so tenacious.

So as you walk through your day, begin to pay attention to your thoughts, feelings, and reactions. What defense mechanisms and types of automatic thoughts can you identify? You might want to make notes about them in a journal so that you can begin to track patterns. As you recognize these, you can ask yourself what beliefs might have led you to these defenses or thoughts. Where might these beliefs have originated in your past? Understanding the architecture of your thoughts will allow you to not only rid yourself of painful and inaccurate beliefs you hold about yourself, others, and circumstances, but it will help you improve the quality of your relationships. You won't get triggered as often and overreact to situations, causing inadvertent conflicts, and you'll be much less likely to make wrong assumptions about the thoughts and feelings of others. You'll no longer perceive their words and behaviors through the filter of your own negative beliefs.

It also helps to realize that others are in the same predicament as you! We all have defense mechanisms, we all have automatic thoughts, and yes, we all have our Innatious intentions.

DEFENSE AND COPING MECHANISMS

Below is a list of some defense and coping mechanisms used to handle stress and anxiety. Try to think of a time in your life when you have used each of them. Make note of the circumstance that caused you to use this particular defense or coping mechanism. Your notes will help you notice future situations in which you jump to use one of these. Don't criticize yourself if you aren't able to catch yourself in the moment and make a different choice. The more aware you become of how these mechanisms operate in your life, the more likely you'll be able to stop them in their tracks and guide your actions based on conscious decisions. But no one manages to catch themselves every time.

Altruism: Excessively helping others in order to feel good about ourselves; concentrating on the pain in others rather than focusing on our own.

Attack: When we feel threatened, even emotionally, attacking back is a common coping mechanism. We may feel stress and lash out at whoever is in our way.

Avoidance: We often seek ways to avoid uncomfortable feelings or situations. For example, let's say you have a conflict with a coworker. Rather than deal with the situation and your feelings about it, you simply avoid walking past their office.

Compartmentalization: We separate one part of ourselves from the awareness of the other part. Example: An oncologist who treats young children with cancer may completely separate her work life from her family life.

Compensation: We make up for a weakness in one area by gaining strength in another. Example: "I may not be good at writing, but I can type 80 wpm." This person compensates for their lack of writing skills with their typing skills.

Denial: We refuse to accept reality because it's too threatening. Example: We may refuse to admit we made a mistake, instead insisting and believing it's someone else's fault.

Displacement: We displace our feelings and impulses onto a more acceptable or less threatening target. Example: We're angry at our spouse but end up being cross with our children as a result.

Intellectualization: We concentrate on the intellectual aspect of a situation, allowing for distance from our emotions. Example: A person who lost a loved one focuses on funeral details to remain distant from the sadness and grief.

Rationalization: We explain our perceptions or behaviors in a logical way in order to avoid our feelings about the reality of the situation. Example: A person demoted from a position they enjoyed reframes the situation like this: "They must not need the position any longer. I wasn't crazy about my responsibilities anyway."

Reaction Formation: We avoid feelings or desires that we perceive to be dangerous or unacceptable, dismissing them as unimportant. Example: You're excited about applying for a new position, but you say the job is no big deal.

Repression: We hide uncomfortable thoughts by pushing them away from our consciousness. Example: A person was abused on a playground but represses the memory. The effects of the abuse come out in pendulaphobia, which is the fear of things that hang and swing,

Passive Aggression: We mask or disguise our feelings of displeasure toward others, and the anger comes out in covert ways. Example: Jan is upset that her friend cancelled their plans. Instead of telling her friend that it upset her, she cancels plans on her friend, while pretending she isn't upset.

Projection: We unconsciously shift unacceptable thoughts and feelings onto another person. Example: Phoebe is jealous of her friend's success, but rather than come to terms with her own jealousy, she accuses her friend of being jealous.

Somatization: We transform uncomfortable feelings into physical symptoms, such as stomach pain or headaches. Example: An executive is restricted in their actions with the Board of Directors and promptly begins to have migraines.

COMMON AUTOMATIC THOUGHTS

Below is a list of some of the most common automatic thoughts. Are any of these familiar to you?

Overgeneralization: A one-time event or situation is now seen as a constant rule. Example: You might say, "My friend stopped calling me. Obviously, people don't like me."

Negative Filtering: Only concentrating on the negatives while not paying attention to any of the positives. Example: You spend a fun night with a friend, but when the friend pokes fun at your outfit, you can't stop thinking about it.

Magnification/Minimization: An exaggeration of negative information, while minimizing positive aspects. Example: Your boss comments that most of your report was great, but there were a few areas that should be corrected. Therefore, you think your report was horrible.

All-or-Nothing Thinking: Thinking in absolutes—black or white, right or wrong, good or bad. Viewing things with no fluctuation. Example: You complain that your supervisor is *always* in a bad mood. "There's *nothing* good about this job!"

Catastrophizing: Expecting the worst to happen. Example: You think, "If I don't land this client, I'm going to get fired."

Emotional Reasoning: Misinterpreting your feelings as facts. Example: You *feel* hopeless. Therefore, you're convinced that your life is hopeless.

Mind Reading: Making assumptions about other people's thoughts without having facts to support them. Example: You might think, "He didn't say he enjoyed our date, so he must have had a bad time."

Fortune Telling Error: Anticipating an outcome and assuming your prediction is factual. (What we believe can be self-fulfilling.) Example: You might say, "I've always been like this, so I won't be able to change" or "I know it isn't going to work out, so there's no point in trying."

Should Statements: Using statements with the word "should" that set the bar high and set up expectations of yourself and others with allowing for change and flexibility. Example: You might say, "I'm a nice person, so no one *should* ever be mean to me."

Labeling: Assigning yourself a negative personality trait and believing it can't change. Example: You might say, "I'm so lazy" or "I'm a hard person to be around."

Personalizing: When you take responsibility for something that you aren't involved in, such as thinking what people say or do is in reaction or related to you. Example: You might say, "My boss is in a bad mood. It must have been something I did. She didn't even look at me when she walked down the hall."

HOW TO CHANGE YOUR AUTOMATIC THOUGHTS

First, become aware of the negative thoughts you're having. Pay attention to any pattern you notice and how often these negative thoughts happen. Once you have identified a regular automatic thought, answer these questions:

1. What are the advantages and disadvantages of this thought?

2. Is this thought objectively true? Do you have evidence to support your negative automatic thought? What is another way of looking at it?

3. If a loved one felt the way you do, what would you say to them?

4. Write down your thoughts and feelings about a situation that upset you. What automatic thought did you have? Can you identify the event that triggered the thought?

5. When you realize which automatic thought(s) you often use, try to stop yourself from saying or thinking them by simply saying in your mind, "STOP!" You may also try wearing a rubber band around your wrist. Each time you have a negative thought, snap the rubber band lightly.

6. Work on replacing the negative thought with a positive thought. For example:

Overgeneralization: Replace "Nobody likes me" with "I get along with most people. My kids, family, and friends like me. I guess not all people are going to like me, but that's okay."

Fortune telling: Replace "My presentation is going be terrible today" with "Even though I'm a bit nervous, I'm going to do my best. I'm as prepared as I can be, and if I can't answer a question, I'll simply say, 'I'm not sure, let me find out and get back to you.'"

6

Living Authentically and Transparently

In the beginning of the book, we talked about Maslow's Hierarchy of Needs. The philosophy is that human beings are trying to reach the top of the pyramid to self-actualization—our continued attempt at growth and development throughout our life to reach our fullest potential.

While striving for self-actualization, two key areas are the ability to live authentically and transparently. Living authentically requires that we become aware of our truth and live as such. Living transparently requires that we allow our authentic self to be seen with nothing we feel we must hide.

It sounds simple, but it isn't. As we grow up, all of the societal requirements chip away at our feelings of security about who we are and what we want. Often, our true self hides underneath layers of negative beliefs, automatic thoughts, and defense mechanisms that have made us feel that our authenticity isn't acceptable. Those beliefs that we aren't good enough prevent us from living transparently.

Think about young children for a moment and their lack of insecurities. They're authentic and transparent to a fault until they learn how to have a societal filter. Of course, authenticity doesn't mean we forego social norms. As adults, we probably aren't going to dance in the middle of a grocery store or belt out a song during a movie in a theater. But as children, society goes far beyond expecting us to adhere to niceties. It pommels us with all kinds of judgments and protocols as to how to behave and be acceptable to others. And our parents tend to raise us based on their own limited beliefs, as well as who they want us to be, perhaps to achieve a future they wanted but didn't attain. So we attempt to fit into the image we feel will keep us accepted by others rather than allow ourselves to remain the person who arrived when we were born. This, unfortunately, can make it very difficult for us to achieve or sustain authenticity and transparency.

That isn't to imply that authenticity is linear; it isn't. Who we are will evolve and change as we grow and mature. We humans are complex, and we must continue to challenge our authenticity and attempt to live transparently based on who we become moment to moment.

Living authentically and transparently is a mindset that requires we stay curious about our internal thoughts and beliefs, as we also acknowledge and honor our feelings. They are two key concepts for understanding our Innatiousness. We have to figure out the true Innatious intention of our actions. Then, we have to adjust those intentions so that they're healthier and in keeping with the truth of who we are and who we want to be. Finally, we may communicate those intentions to others for greater freedom and satisfying relationships. Incorporating Innatious is how we become authentic and transparent.

Living authentically and transparently is a life-long process. Hopefully, we learn more every day about how to do it. It's important to remember, however, that self-awareness isn't a destination; it's a journey toward living our truth. It's the gift of being yourself and finding your greatest happiness. And authenticity and transparency are necessary for true fulfillment and contentment.

THE COST OF INAUTHENTICITY

If we don't know our Innatiousness and how to fulfill our LAR needs, it may set us on a journey of less than fulfilling relationships and career aspirations. How many people attend medical school or law school because they were told it would ensure financial success, only to discover years later that they feel no satisfaction in their profession because it hasn't been authentic to them? Money buys choices, not happiness.

There are large numbers of people who live someone else's life based on what they believe they "should" do. They know they're unhappy, but they don't know why because they've never investigated the source of the problem.

For example, Paul grew up with four brothers and the assumption that he would become part of the family business as soon as he was old enough. All of the men in his family had become auto mechanics for three generations. No one had ever dared to try a different profession. Only the women in the family seemed to be allowed to do anything else.

While in school, Paul discovered that he had both a love and an aptitude for biology. One of his high school teachers encouraged him to pursue it, but he didn't feel he could possibly go against his family's expectations. His Innatious intent in this situation was to avoid conflict and not risk disappointing his father, grandfather, and brothers. If he disappointed them, he feared he would lose their love. But because of those fears, he sacrificed his authenticity. It was a long-term price to pay for what would have probably been a short-term argument.

Poet David Whyte has said that if we live authentically—pursuing the life we truly want—that someone in our life will probably feel betrayed. Many people never take the risk of possibly betraying or disappointing a parent or someone else in their life, so they stay stuck in life-long self-betrayal.

If Paul had thought about his purpose in life and what he wanted to be known for, he might have been able to break away from the confines of his upbringing and do what he really wanted.

Take me as an example. I want to be known as an expert in human behavior and behavior change. I had four older sisters and was quite the observer. We were all so very different, and I wanted to understand why. I watched the struggles of my parents and my sisters in relationships and could see communication gaps. It was clear that their drivers (the *why*) for being in many of these relationships were unhealthy.

My desire to understand led me to become a psychologist. My father, a successful entrepreneur, was proud I was going to college, but wasn't crazy about my career choice. He believed

I was limiting myself, so he challenged me by saying I would never be as financially successful as he. His reverse psychology worked in a way. I was going to live as my authentic self and become a psychologist, but his challenge weighed me down a bit in the early part of my career. My Innatious driver was to make my dad proud of me, and maybe along the way, prove to myself that I was right by living my passion. The fruits of my many years of training, insights, and lessons learned are captured in this book. Connecting with our purpose in life and how we'd like to be known or remembered can help us connect with our authentic self.

Then, of course, there's inauthenticity in our relationships. There are people who look for the "right" partner based on an image they've adopted from their parents or society, only to realize that the relationship doesn't work for who they truly are underneath it all.

That was the case for Mavis. She grew up with the belief that the best partner would be someone with a lot of money and prestige. So she married a man who fit that profile and satisfied both her parents. She was the envy of all of her friends, as she went on expensive vacations and lived in a gorgeous home. But to do this, she had to pretend to be someone she was not. At first, she wasn't aware that she was pretending, but over time, the façade began to crack. Her true self wanted to come out.

Her initial Innatious intent was to not disappoint her parents. Then, it morphed into the intention to be envied by others in order to build up her own lack of self-esteem. She thought she would feel important and loved if she married someone who was high-profile and wealthy. But as she grew older, she began to feel her own worth, and her Innatious intent matured as she did. She no longer felt the need to impress others, so the reason for her choice of partner gradually disappeared. As a result, she began to see her marriage more realistically. She started to explore her own inner life, which made her realize that her relationship was superficial.

Luckily for Mavis, she was able to embrace her authenticity and become more transparent with her husband. She was surprised to learn that he was willing to work on their relationship and deepen their intimacy. They entered couples therapy and began to talk about their true feelings. Each strived to show the other who they really were, and while there were some rocky times during the process, they were able to be vulnerable and see each other without judgment. They decided to start over, make compromises, and find a new way of being with each other that allowed each of them to be fully themselves.

Then, there's Irene, who told me, "I don't feel I have any idea who I am anymore. I've been a mom for so long that it became my whole identity. Everything I did was in relation to someone else. Now that they've left the nest, who is this person in the mirror?" When Irene explored the Innatious intent behind her devotion to motherhood, she discovered that she held a belief that the only way to be a good mother was to abandon her own needs. She also believed that she wouldn't be a good person unless she was a good mother. So her Innatious driver was to be a good, worthy person. The role fulfilled her for a while until slowly, as her kids aged, she began feeling the effects of her abandonment as she grew and her Innatiousness changed.

What she didn't realize was that it would have been possible to lead a more balanced life, taking excellent care of her children, while also allowing herself to be authentic and take care of her own needs at the same time. She certainly might have made compromises from one day to the next, but not 24 hours a day, seven days a week for the full length of her children's lives. She could have included time for herself. After all, it's advantageous for parents to show their children how to maintain balance. This teaches them problem-solving and coping skills as well, as they watch their parents negotiate ways to balance all of the demands in life. It also teaches children compromise and how to balance their own needs with the needs of others.

But once Irene's children were adults, she didn't know what to do with herself and felt disconnected from her true self. She had to begin to explore what she loved and determine how she'd like to fill her time. It took some effort, but eventually, she rediscovered a love of writing and started composing articles for a friend's magazine. That led to assignments with other magazines, and before she knew it, she had a sense of purpose in her life that used her talents well. She no longer centered her life around her husband and children, and her marriage even improved because she allowed herself to have the Innatious intent of authenticity, transparency, and personal fulfillment.

The bottom line is that we can only become authentic if we understand what drives us, what frightens us, what feelings we may be trying to avoid, and how to better manage our emotions.

While balance is an ideal that we don't achieve every moment of our lives, if you find yourself feeling emotional extremes, it's time to examine what's happening under the surface. Think about a retro weight and balance scale. Your goal is to try to keep it as steady in the center as possible. Sometimes it will lean more to the right, and sometimes more to the left, but overall, it should balance out. You can use this metaphor when thinking about your work schedule, relationships, diet, drinking habits, and just about anything else. Any area of life that is one-sided may end up tipping the scale over, just as it did for Irene.

HOW DO YOU KNOW IF YOU'RE LIVING AUTHENTICALLY AND TRANSPARENTLY?

When we aren't authentic or transparent, we often compart-mentalize our life, placing issues into the back of our minds so that we can avoid dealing with them. Sometimes, we do this consciously, and sometimes we don't realize we're concealing it from ourselves. Through using these defense mechanisms, we protect our vulnerabilities rather than face them. Often, people hide vulnerability because they fear it makes them appear weak.

But this lack of authenticity creates a great deal of stress. Whatever we feel we must hide causes tension as we strive desperately to keep it hidden. The fear that we'll be "found out" (again, whether conscious or unconscious) churns under the surface as we go about our lives, trying to pretend to ourselves and others that nothing is wrong. But this kind of stress can cause eruptions in relationships, emotional upheaval, and even physical illness. We rob ourselves of the peace and freedom that authenticity and transparency can bring.

Ask yourself how much you hide from others. It's certainly your right to be private, and your life is no one else's business. The differences may be subtle, but authenticity and transparency are something beyond privacy. It's the areas where we choose to be private that may inhibit our authenticity and happiness—areas like communication in relationships, who we love, and what we do for a living. When we're inauthentic or feel we can't be transparent, there is some insecurity such as the fear that others will judge us. If you disagree with this statement, that others will judge you, but you don't feel it necessary to tell people "your stuff," ask yourself why that is. Dig deep—what concerns you about letting people really see you? Saying "because it's my business" is a cop out. Again, you don't actually have to tell anyone anything, but knowing why you don't want to be transparent is important.

When you truly have nothing to hide, you accept yourself, even with all of your foibles and the mistakes you've made in the past. Then, you can relax when you're with others because there's nothing you feel you have to work to hide. Your life may be private, but if someone finds out about some aspect of your private life, it won't be a source of shame for you. And for true intimacy with those you're closest to, you need to be transparently yourself. If you can share everything about yourself in your closest relationships, you'll feel a sense of safety that's beyond anything you've experienced before.

So what's holding you back from living your truth? What fears are in the way, and what specifically is your Innatious intent in hiding? If you don't feel there are any insecurities and that your life is great, it's healthy to occasionally *lean in* to some insecurities that might be underneath your awareness and explore them. We do annual health checkups even when we feel great, for example. So doing an annual emotional check-in is an equally healthy action. It's important as we age to reflect on our experiences.

You can see a therapist or even just have discussions with an insightful friend—someone you trust and who challenges you, but without judgment. Reach out to them, and schedule a coffee. Have a deeper and richer conversation about life by asking each other more "why" questions. It isn't so much about your opinions, but *why* you hold those opinions. What are the origins of those opinions? Sometimes, when we discover the "why" we believe something (our Innatiousness), we realize it isn't a viable opinion at all.

For example, let's say you believe you aren't capable of advancing any further in your career. Your friend tries to convince you that you're wrong. When you explore the "why" of your belief/opinion, you discover that it probably goes back to your childhood, when your mother told you not to set your sights too high so that you wouldn't be disappointed. She thought she was protecting you, but her belief became your own and ultimately held you back. Once you recall what your mother said, you realize it's her own belief in limitation, not your own, that's preventing you from striving further. This realization puts you on solid ground to reframe your long-held belief, so you can begin working to push yourself past your comfort zone and see just how far you can go.

During your discussion with your friend, you might talk about what bugs you in your life and why you think it bugs you. You may even ask how this person and others view you. Make an agreement that you won't become defensive. Instead, be curious about what you may be doing that could use some alteration. For example, perhaps some of your friends feel you talk too much and monopolize conversations. Your Innatious intent in that situation is to feel heard and understood. Maybe as a child, you felt that your parents didn't hear or understand you enough, so you've inadvertently overcompensated for it as an adult. While you might not be able to immediately feel more heard and understood, you could rectify the situation by setting a timer when talking to friends so that you don't go on for too long. You could become more mindful of asking your friends to talk about themselves and work on deepening your listening skills.

Here's another example: Your friend tells you that you sometimes come across to others as a "know-it-all." This wouldn't be a fun thing to hear, but you could use this information to begin to alter your behavior. What would be your Innatious intention when you behave this way? Perhaps you want to appear smart because one of your insecurities is that you *aren't* smart. Once you're aware of this Innatious intention, you can work on strengthening your belief in your intelligence so that you don't feel the need to prove it to others. This will help you behave more authentically without the restrictions that your insecurity has placed on your behavior.

Here are some other questions you can ask yourself to determine if you've been less than authentic and transparent:

- Do you feel you're avoiding something, such as a belief, desire, fear, rejection, or love?

- Do you fear at times that a truth about you will come out in the open?

- Have you misled anyone in your life?

- Does your concern about what others think of you prevent you from being yourself?

- Do you believe your strengths are good enough?

- Do you accept your weaknesses and mistakes without getting down on yourself?

- Do you have your emotional guard up with people who love you?

- Are you able to voluntary apologize to someone you wronged?

- Do you feel confused about who are you?

- Do you feel confused about a relationship?

- Do you pretend to be someone you aren't or feel something you don't?

- Do you hold back negative information from others?

- Do you often embellish stories?

- Do you get upset when someone questions your behavior or thoughts?

- Do you think you can handle your own issues without help?

- Is it difficult for you to access your feelings or talk about them?

- Are there relationships in your life that you wish were better?

Most of us could probably say "yes" to at least one of these questions (if we're honest), so this is certainly not an opportunity to put yourself down or feel that you're somehow inferior because you have more to work on within yourself. Join the club! As I said, self-awareness isn't a destination. There is never an end to what we can discover about our inner life. But that doesn't have to feel like work. It can be a fascinating life journey. The fact that we're complex beings is something to celebrate.

So if you answered "yes" to any or many of these, consider each as simply an opportunity to examine how you can become more authentic and transparent in your life. At the end of the chapter, you'll find an exercise to help you explore issues like these further and how they apply to your specific circumstances.

AUTHENTICITY AND EMPATHY

Living our truth is aspirational. It doesn't mean we abandon our empathy for others. On the contrary, we must integrate empathy while living our truth. What does this mean? Although we may be living our truth, we must be cautious not to inhibit another person's journey. Our goal is to live our truth and let others explore and find themselves so they may live their truth.

Also, transparency doesn't mean we verbalize every thought we have. It makes sense to hold back what we think or feel if it serves no purpose other than to hurt someone else. We don't want to force our subjective thoughts and opinions on someone else, especially when not requested. We must also consider when we have an opinion that's negative—is it coming from our own insecurities to make us feel better about ourselves?

Authenticity and the freedom and joy it cultivates don't mean you're immune from feeling hurt by someone else's opinion about you. You're human, and your feelings are real—being authentic means you acknowledge even those feelings you wish you didn't have. So instead of judging yourself for any negative feelings you have about yourself, work on managing your reactions. Guard against shutting down from what you feel in the moment. Consider the evidence of those feelings, and adjust and reframe the automatic thoughts and beliefs behind them. Move yourself through the feelings to the healthiest response you can have.

Authenticity enhances our capacity for empathy because we aren't as easily triggered by issues that bring up our insecurities. When we're authentic and transparent, we trust ourselves and who we are. And when we understand the work involved with being authentic and transparent, we're much more likely to empathize with others as they work on it, too. Then, when we fall back into destructive patterns and question our authentic selves, we catch ourselves and take the time to look at our Innatious intentions and make adjustments. That helps to prevent us from taking the actions of others personally so that we can strive to understand their point of view and whatever Innatiousness may be driving their behavior. When we can do that, our relationships are more fulfilling, both because we feel loved for the person we truly are and because we're able to love someone else for who they truly are.

The bottom line is this: The more we ask ourselves the "why" and continue asking it until a lightbulb goes off, the faster and easier we will make positive changes in our life and in our relationships.

AUTHENTICITY AND TRANSPARENCY EXERCISE

The following are additional questions you may ask yourself in order to bring more awareness to potential barriers to living your most authentic and transparent life. These are deep questions that may unearth some difficult information from your unconscious. If so, you may feel it necessary to discuss these questions and your answers with a therapist, coach, or at least a non-judgmental and insightful friend. A professional, however, is probably your best option for the support you'll need to go deeper within. The benefits of this exploration are enormous—as an authentic and transparent life is the foundation of contentment and fulfillment.

1. What, if anything, are you hiding from someone you love? What is your Innatious intention in hiding it? Is that intention based on a fear or belief? If so, do you have an idea when this fear or belief may have originated? Is the belief inherently true, or just something you've come to accept as truth?

2. Think of a situation at work, at home, or socially when you pretended to be someone you're not. Write about this situation, and then reread what you've written. Can you recognize your Innatious intent to embellish yourself?

3. Imagine behaving without pretense in the situation you just wrote about. What do you think would have happened? Does it frighten you to think of being your true self in this situation? If so, why?

4. What weaknesses and mistakes do you judge yourself for the most? Can you imagine forgiving and accepting yourself for them? Close your eyes, and picture yourself accepting yourself in all of your humanness. What does that feel like? Can you envision that possibility? What would it take to accept yourself as you truly are?

5. Is there anyone in your life to whom you owe an apology? What is your Innatious intent in withholding that apology? What would it take for you to offer it?

6. When was the last time you embellished a story you told? Write down the true story. Then, write down the embellishment you added. What was your Innatious intent in adding the embellishment?

7. Think of a situation or relationship in your life that troubles you. Can you access your feelings about it? Have you been able to discuss your feelings about it with the people involved? If not, have you discussed your feelings with a disinterested party? If you're truly authentic and transparent in this situation or relationship, what do you think will happen? What do you fear the most? What do you believe would be the best solution to the problem?

7

Changing Assumptions and Judgments

Marlene has a strong Innatious need to feel useful and appear knowledgeable to others, which helps her feel good about herself. As a result, she has a tendency to tell people what to do, assuming that she knows what's best for them. This has caused many arguments in her relationships with friends and family members. They don't take kindly to being told what to do, and they especially dislike it when Marlene acts like she's the authority on their life.

What they don't realize is that this behavior comes from a deep insecurity that developed when Marlene was a child. She internalized her parents' behavior to mean that she was stupid and useless. Her parents didn't mean to make her feel that way, but they tended to do everything for her, including helping her with her homework as if she wasn't capable of doing it herself.

Their Innatious intent was to be good, helpful parents, not realizing that they were preventing their daughter from gaining confidence in her own abilities.

As a result of this, Marlene has often overcompensated for this belief about herself by asserting her knowledge in an overpowering way. When she was able to unearth the issue, she realized that she had accomplished much in her life that proved she was useful and knowledgeable. She didn't need to work so hard to make sure others thought so. Actually, they already did. She also discovered that she had inadvertently been doing to others what her parents had done to her—infantilizing them rather than allowing them to make their own decisions and mistakes.

Still, changing her behavior wasn't easy. Telling people what to do and acting like she knew best were habitual behaviors to fill her unconscious Innatious need. Marlene had to work hard to chip away at this habit. Her newfound awareness will allow for the process of change.

Why is change so difficult? Because of the nature of the subconscious and unconscious parts of our mind, as well as the development of beliefs, automatic thoughts, and behaviors in childhood. As children, we don't have the cognitive ability to judge circumstances realistically. So we make many wrong assumptions about what we observe and experience. For example, if a parent says, "What's wrong with you?" in anger, we take it literally, internalizing that something is indeed inherently wrong with us. We don't realize that our parents have their own insecurities and Innatiousness to contend with.

Assumptions like these are made instinctually rather than through conscious thought, and as a result, they're ingrained in us. What we learn as children molds the way we perceive the world, and we internalize many of our parents' and community's beliefs without realizing it. The beliefs and automatic thoughts from our childhood make up our foundation, and our foundational beliefs largely come from our family culture, which is inclusive of our religion, ethnicity, family size, and makeup. Needless to say, change can be very complex. Therefore, it's a process—a long-term adjustment.

The key to changing anything about ourselves is to first become aware of the behavior or reaction we want to change. How do we become aware of it? If we have an uncomfortable feeling, we tend to blame it on some external factor. Instead, we can ask: What need is not being met? Why do we feel this way? Where is it coming from? These questions are pointed toward us, not the external factor.

If you catch yourself saying something like, "It's just the way I'm wired," take a moment to self-reflect, and think about your Innatiousness. Once you begin the process of awareness, you can work toward change. You can then begin to catch yourself and adjust your reactions and responses accordingly. The basic cycle of change is (1) awareness, (2) catching yourself during or after the behavior, and (3) eventually catching yourself *before* the behavior so that you can change it by making a new choice.

For Marlene, the process of change meant first becoming aware of her behavior and Innatious intent. Once she knew why she was telling others what to do and her Innatious intent to feel more secure in her own intelligence, she could begin to catch herself "in the act." In the beginning, she wasn't quite able to stop, but she observed herself in the middle of the behavior. She hated to see it, especially that she was now aware of how much it bothered the other people in her life. And she developed a new understanding of their feelings and potential Innatiousness in the situation.

Over time, she was more and more able to catch herself *before* she started to tell someone what to do with their life. It wasn't easy, but she learned to bite her tongue and enhance her listening skills. This led to a greater understanding of what the other person was trying to express. Sometimes, she opted to offer an opinion, but from a much softer perspective. Rather than present her idea as the only viable option, she offered it as a possibility for the other person to consider.

Even after working on this issue for a few years, Marlene still finds that she has to be vigilant. The habit is tenacious, and if she's tired or emotionally triggered, she can fall back into her old behavior, getting caught in it once again.

The process of change is an inside-out endeavor that, without question, takes time, self-reflection, repetition, patience, and persistence to integrate the new behavior or reaction, one step at a time. And understanding our Innatiousness is at the core!

THE *SCHEMA* CONCEPT

There is a concept that psychologists use to describe our pattern of thoughts that organize and categorize old and new information. It's called a *schema*. This information is gathered from the time of our birth. Schemas are useful as they build a framework that allows us to interpret things quickly and even automatically at times. Basically, schemas help us make sense of things.

But we categorize situations from our preexisting beliefs and ideas, and we instinctually want to be right. In fact, research shows that our brains release dopamine, a chemical that makes us feel better, when we feel we're right about something. Conversely, when we learn we're wrong about anything, we feel worse. So we look for answers anywhere and everywhere to justify our decisions. This, of course, means that our schemas can be faulty or downright false.

Our schemas basically create a blueprint of the information we believe to be true, and we select information from our environment based on our anticipated schematic reference. This means we only see what we know to look for, and as a result, we fail to integrate all of the facts and information available to us. For example, stereotyping—a non-empathetic and oversimplified way to characterize a person or group of people—is a common result of this phenomenon. We take our experiences and the interpretations of others who believe the same as we do, and we see the world through a skewed view that validates our own internal thoughts.

Are there truths in stereotyping? Perhaps, but this discussion is not about whether stereotyping is bad, good, or indifferent. It's simply about acknowledging it and understanding where it comes from. Again, we can only change what we bring to awareness.

To put this chapter in context, let's focus on the negative aspect of judging, such as when it turns into a prejudice. Technically, the definition of prejudice is an opinion that isn't based on reason, but is a belief connected to our values.

Sometimes, thoughts come to mind automatically, even when we don't consciously agree with those thoughts. For example, what's your initial reaction when you see a person who looks perfectly healthy getting into their parked car in a disabled spot? You may know intellectually that not all disabilities are visible, but it might still take time and practice for you to avoid automatically jumping to your preconceived notion.

Here's another example: An interviewer at a company has a belief that women aren't as adept in executive positions as men. The interviewer may be completely unaware of this belief, but he unconsciously makes hiring decisions as a result of it. Even if a woman is more qualified, he will be more likely to choose a man to fill a position because of his preexisting belief. This belief could have been formed in childhood. Perhaps he internalized it from his parents, even if they never came out and said such a thing, or his Innatious intent might be to feel superior as a man because he has an unconscious belief that he's inferior.

Of course, we're all aware of racial and gender prejudices. A 2017 Harvard Business School study found that Asian and African American job applicants were more likely to get a job interview if they masked their race on their resumes. Similarly, a 2019 study published in *Educational Researcher* showed that teachers tend to assume girls have lower math abilities than boys. Many of the people with these prejudices are unaware of them.

Unfortunately, human cultures tend to see the world in terms of black and white, right or wrong, success or failure, normal or not normal. We tend to avoid shades of gray, even though the reality of human existence is that it's far from cut and dry, and there are actually an infinite number of gray shades.

Why do we do this? Simplifying matters to either/or gives us the illusion of control. It's less scary to see the world in these terms because then, we believe we can more easily come up with an answer to the problems we face. This makes us feel more stable and less anxious. But this thinking doesn't take into account the nuance that exists in life, and it often fosters intolerance and judgments of both ourselves and others.

Why do you think we hold such prejudices, sometimes unconsciously? What's the intent in thinking negatively about someone else? When we peel the layers back on our thoughts, we can say that such judgments help us feel better about ourselves. Sometimes, we judge someone because we're fearful and need to justify that fear and the resulting behavior. Our insecurities are eased when we project our inner negativity onto another person, just like the man who unconsciously judges women as less capable in order to feel better about himself as a man.

We make decisions at every turn; there's no avoiding it. We make judgment calls, consciously or unconsciously, all the time—judging a situation is how we get through the day. Our interpretation of a situation can happen very fast, pulling from past experiences and associations that may no longer be relevant. How do we then sift out if our judgment is *accurate*? When we determine the Innatious intent of a judgment, we have the opportunity to respond more precisely. But we also have to guard against judging our own behavior before we investigate the *why* behind it. It's human to make mistakes and snap judgments.

For example, it may be very unpleasant for the man mentioned above to uncover that he judges women as ill-equipped to handle technical jobs because the judgment helps him feel superior. Again, his Innatious intent is to feel better about himself due to his deep-seated insecurity. That insecurity may have developed as a result of issues with his mother from childhood, which created an association with all women that he then projects onto them. But once he's brought that to awareness, dealt with his feelings about it, and understood his Innatious intent, he can begin to work on his underlying insecurity and build his self-confidence. The result will not only be increased confidence, but also less internal tension and better relationships with women.

Here are more examples: A woman may have had so many negative experiences with men that she comes to judge all men as untrustworthy. Or someone might think of all wealthy people as superficial and greedy.

One of the tasks of emotional intelligence is to teach ourselves to react differently from these prejudices, which may manifest as knee-jerk reactions. When we have these automatic thoughts, we have to stop them in their tracks and refuse to stay there. We have to assess each individual situation on its specific merits. We have to ask ourselves what we Innatiously need. What feelings are we avoiding, or what do we need to feel? For example, the woman who has come to believe that all men are untrustworthy may have the Innatious intent to feel safe. She has been hurt, so by assuming all men can't be trusted, she believes she's protecting herself from future hurt. But in doing so, she's also preventing herself from possibly meeting a man who *is* trustworthy and entering into a friendship or loving relationship with him.

The more we ask ourselves the important and difficult questions, the more we'll become aware of our thoughts, as well as understand why these thoughts have come up. This, in turn, creates a better understanding of who we are, how we relate to others, and how our Innatiousness impacts us and our relationships. And remember: there are always two Innatious intentions in any given relationship or interaction between two people.

Of course, we can't alleviate all of our judgments. We'll always have them from both a positive and a negative place. The key is to recognize the judgment and determine the Innatious intention behind it. Is it to feed our ego, to make a better decision, or to comfort ourselves?

INTERPRETATIONS, PERCEPTIONS, AND BIASES

Our perceptions are based on our experiences and basic senses. Through our perceptions, we acquire, interpret, select, and organize information. We're in a constant state of perceiving, and we use available information in the environment to direct our actions. But we frequently misinterpret the information we receive, causing us to perceive situations incorrectly.

Think of a silhouette of a person in a dark alley. Through their schematic process, one person may categorize the figure as a man with a baseball bat, perceiving the situation as scary. Another person might categorize the figure as an older lady with a cane, perceiving it as non-threatening.

Here's another thought-provoking example: You see a dark spot on the wall from across the room. Someone with a particular schematic reference may perceive it as a spider (that would be mine). Others might immediately think it's a crack in the paint on the wall.

PERCEPTION WORKSHEET

Below are two well-known pictures on deciphering perceptions. What do you see?

Picture 1

- What do you see?

- Do you see an elderly lady?

- Do you see a younger lady?

- Do you see both?

- Which did you see first?

Picture 2

- What do you see?

- Do you see the profile of a person with glasses?

- Do you see a word written out in cursive?

- Do you see the word "liar"?

- Which did you see first?

These are just two of many examples of perceptions and how we all interpret things differently. Now, consider how these interpretations play a part in our cultural, religious, political, and other beliefs.

This automatic thought process is how we manage life and make quick decisions. In fact, our brains are programmed for it. We have to process so much information every day that we couldn't possibly do it all consciously. So our unconscious mind is constantly busy, looking for recognizable patterns in order to interpret what we see, hear, and experience. Our tendency to make quick interpretations is even more pronounced when we're stressed, tired, or ill.

It's an aspect of the fight-or-flight response, which human beings have needed throughout time to survive. The human instinct doesn't discriminate when that response occurs. We evaluate situations with our personal survival in mind, and we react quickly without conscious thought. It's a brain shortcut in order to keep us out of harm's way. When we have a fight-or-flight response, our Innatiousness is all about staying safe. So we interpret or perceive situations and people based largely on our Innatiousness.

Luckily, however, we do have the power of thought, contemplation, and processing to go beyond that response and perceive the world from a more reasonable, factual perspective. Without discovering our Innatiousness and the *why* of our beliefs and automatic thoughts, we fail to use these conscious, cognitive abilities to evaluate our experiences. Instead, we fall prey to our unconscious biases.

We like to think we aren't biased about anything, but most all of us have experienced unconscious bias of some kind from both sides of the coin. And bias is largely responsible for our perceptions and interpretations. The operative word is "unconscious." We aren't aware that we're biased until we pay attention. Only then can we make changes that allow us to perceive situations based on truth rather than our snap judgments and assumptions.

Psychologists have identified more than 150 different types of unconscious bias, but here are some of the most common types:

Confirmation Bias: This is the bias that leads us to look for evidence that corroborates what we already believe. This bias also causes us to disregard evidence that contradicts what we already believe. Businessman Warren Buffet once said, "What the human being is best at doing is interpreting all new information so that their prior conclusions remain intact." Remember that our brains release a feel-good chemical when we believe we're right.

Let's say you send someone a text, and they don't respond for a few days. You already have a fearful belief that you aren't likable, so confirmation bias causes you to assume the other person's lack of response is because they don't like you. As you become more and more convinced that you've lost this friend, you disregard past evidence that this person is fond of you. If the person does finally respond, saying they were out of town or at a hospital, you may realize that their lack of response had nothing to do with you.

As you peel the onion on Innatiousness, you must go deeper to ask yourself why you would make the non-response about you. This is an instance where Innatious is a negative feeling, but it still provides the benefit of an answer to the void of the unresponsive text. It feels out of control not to know why your texts are going unanswered; therefore, you create an assumption to decrease the anxiety of the unknown.

In a relationship, you might be irritated by the fact that your partner has been late on a couple of occasions. Confirmation Bias, however, would cause you to affirm that your partner is *always* late, while you ignore the times he/she has been on time.

Does the evidence support your bias? When you use Innatious, it enables you to ask the question, "Is my partner being disrespectful of my time, or am I being extra sensitive because I've allowed multiple people to do this?" Your Innatiousness is about you, and in a negative aspect (which most biases lean toward), not having to own that you have enabled people to disrespect you. It's about not setting boundaries.

Similar-to-Me Bias: This bias causes us to feel most comfortable with people who are like us. While there's nothing inherently wrong with that, it limits our understanding of the wider world. We might also choose partners and friends based less on their true attributes than simply because they seem to be more like us. For example, you might like the way someone dresses or agrees with you on an issue, so you make assumptions that it means they're like you in other ways. Your Innatiousness with Similar-to-Me bias is most likely two-fold: to feel comfortable and safe with the people you encounter and to avoid the discomfort of feeling different.

When we choose people from a more conscious and objective viewpoint without fear, however, our decisions are more likely to be healthy.

Beauty Bias: This bias rewards people for their physical attractiveness and may cause us to ascribe qualities to them that go beyond their physicality. For example, we may want to be friends with someone because they are better than average looking, so we assume they're also successful, popular, perhaps intelligent, and/or kind. But physical appearance has nothing to do with any of those other attributes. Conversely, we may assume the exact opposite of someone we perceive as unattractive, thinking automatically that they are *not* successful, popular, or intelligent.

Our surface level desire may be to simply choose great friends. If this bias is present, we wrongly assume someone is great or not just because of how they look. As we integrate the Innatious intent, we find out that this bias was, of course, about us, and that we may appear more attractive, intelligent, successful, or popular to others by virtue of our attractive friends.

Attribution Bias: This bias causes us to attribute our accomplishments to our own hard work or skills, while we attribute our failures to things we have no control over. With others, however, we sometimes perceive their successes as luck, while we believe their failures are a result of their own lack of skills, lack of hard work, or lack of positive personal qualities.

With Innatious, remember, we're trying to identify the *why* behind the feeling. It isn't easy because with bias, we're avoiding an uncomfortable feeling by justifying our shortcomings or elevating our sense of self. Certainly, we have every right to feel proud of our accomplishments and recognize our hard work and skills. But when we justify or overinflate our sense of self, this can be a blind side to seeing our Innatious drivers. So what is the Innatiousness when we fail, and our bias is to believe it wasn't our fault? When we fail, it's uncomfortable. Therefore, we search for ways to make ourselves feel better (Innatious).

What is the Innatiousness when we dilute someone else's success to mere luck rather than skill? The feeling here may be jealousy or envy. The question is, what drives us to be jealous of what the other person has? It could be as simple as that the accolades they received were a trigger because we didn't get that recognition from our parents. Or it could be as complicated as feelings of disappointment because a parent told us we would never amount to anything. Innatious is the personal quest to get to the next level of what drives us and why we think and behave as we do.

Feelings that are triggered by bias might short-circuit us from getting to a deeper understanding of our Innatious drivers. This doesn't mean that our initial feelings are invalid, but we often need to go deeper. Identifying Innatiousness within our biases is difficult, as biases help us avoid uncomfortable feelings about ourselves. If we begin to identify our biases, however, the reward can be a deeper understanding of our Innatious drivers.

AWARENESS OF YOUR INNATIOUSNESS

Again, awareness is the key to any kind of change or adjustment in our lives, and knowing our Innatiousness helps us in every instance. The more experiences we have, the more we build our schemas, and the more likelihood our perceptions will change. This then causes our Innatiousness to change.

Granted, self-awareness can be painful. It isn't easy to acknowledge our biases. The desire to be right is one of the main reasons why we stay in denial and develop defense mechanisms. Self-awareness requires humility and a willingness to see ourselves realistically, even if it isn't always pretty. The rewards of this work, however, are simply too great to stay locked in the tension of denial.

Understanding our Innatiousness helps us perceive people and situations more accurately, as we also recognize and acknowledge the Innatiousness of others. Since our perceptions sometimes clash with others, it also helps in many situations to communicate our Innatiousness with others and hear theirs, when possible. As we understand the Innatiousness of each other, we learn to feel more empathetic, which helps us to improve our relationships and reduce the hold that our judgments and biases have had on us.

BIAS EXPLORATION

Answer the following questions:

1. Can you think of a situation in your life in which you had Confirmation Bias or when you someone imposed this bias on you? Write about it in your journal.

2. When in your life have you been guilty of Similar-to-Me Bias? Write about it in your journal.

3. Have you ever experienced Beauty Bias? If so, write about it in your journal.

4. Can you think of a time in your life when you were guilty of Attribution Bias, or have you experienced it from someone else? If so, write about it in your journal.

5. What insights have you learned from exploring your own biases, and how will you work to change them so that you're more truthful with yourself and others?

8

Can You Be Friends With An Ex?

Carol and Tom had always had an easygoing relationship. They rarely argued throughout their 17-year marriage. They had always enjoyed their time together and had a lot in common. They read the same books, loved the same films and theater, and they were aligned on social and political issues. The one issue they didn't quite agree on however, was how to raise their family. Tom was a bit more traditional when it came to gender roles and chores. Carol succumbed to most of Tom's desires when it came to how to raise their twins, Madison and Matthew, but she made one major compromise that ultimately took a toll on her. She took a break from work when she had children.

When the children were five years old, Carol had always planned to go back to her career in marketing and sales. Tom knew this, but he always hoped that she would stay home until the kids were at least in high school. He imagined that after being home with them, she would enjoy it too much to stop. But as the kids reached their school years, Carol began researching the job market. Meanwhile, Tom convinced her to become active in the kids' school and extracurricular activities. He thought she would be able to use her marketing skills for their many plays, sports teams, booster clubs, PTA, and fundraisers while also attending to the children's needs.

As the children reached middle school, however, Tom and Carol's relationship had become more platonic than romantic. They established a routine. Tom would go to work, make it to most of the kids' events, and have dinner with the family. Carol ensured the house was maintained, that her family had all they needed, and that dinner was on the table every night. Then, she awoke one day to realize her kids were shopping for their college dorm rooms. In that moment, she had an epiphany and realized she no longer wanted to be married to Tom. She loved him, but she hadn't been *in love* with him for several years. She wanted the freedom to make her own choices and fulfill her own needs without having to consider what Tom wanted or needed.

Even though she and Tom had much in common, Carol was an extrovert who loved to travel and socialize with friends. Tom was more of an introvert who built his life around his family and work. Carol had always planned most of their social activities with friends, so she was an important influence on his social life outside of work.

Over the next couple of years, Carol made the decision to separate. She and Tom tried counseling but realized their goals for the next chapter of their lives were drastically different. Carol also realized that her LAR scores had gotten so low that she had no energy or desire to work on increasing the scores within the relationship.

Ultimately, the separation was amenable, but Tom treated the day-to-day as if nothing had changed. In the beginning, they continued to go to dinner and the movies, and they talked about their interests and current events a couple times per week. Tom called or texted Carol at least once a day. She was fine with having him in her life, but she was also building a new life with new friends.

As Carol gradually communicated with Tom less and saw her new friends more, he became prone to bouts of extreme loneliness. He was worried that without Carol, he would isolate himself and become depressed. He called her, told her he missed her, and wanted to know if they could work things out. While he did love Carol, Tom's Innatious intention in trying to get back with her was to avoid being lonely. He had always struggled to make friends, so he wanted to avoid the stress of that necessity.

Although Carol loved her new life, she also knew Tom wasn't socializing, and their children told her how alone and sad he was. So she agreed to spend more time with him. Her Innatious intent was to avoid the guilt of his loneliness and the upset it was causing her kids.

What do you think will end up happening for Tom and Carol? Can we *really* be friends with our ex?

When asking people this question, I have received answers all across the board. Most people have said they think we can be friends depending on the circumstances of the breakup.

Ultimately, I don't disagree, but let's dig a little deeper as to the various reasons why we might want to remain friends after the ending of an intimate relationship.

We've explored the Innatiousness of Carol and Tom, but there are likely different Innatious intentions for remaining friends with an ex, whether we initiated the breakup or not. In either scenario, however, understanding our Innatious intention helps us determine if the decision to stay friends is healthy. If so, what boundaries are needed for the connection to *remain* healthy and in balance?

Remember that our Innatious intent is always about getting some need met. Some might simply say, "I just want to be friends. We have a history together and enjoy each other's company. So why wouldn't we stay friends?" Yes, it's possible that our Innatious intent is that we just enjoy spending time with our ex and still have much in common. It's hard to give up someone who knows us so well and with whom we've developed trust and security.

This rationale is reasonable when the Innatious intention of both parties is truly to just be friends with no strings attached. But many times after a breakup, one party doesn't want the romantic relationship to end.

What might be the Innatious intent of the one who did the breaking up? We can refer to this person as the "break-upper." Since this person made the decision to sever the relationship, they would more than likely have emotional control in the situation and be ready to move on to date others. In addition, they would likely be okay if their ex moved on and formed a new relationship. Their adjustment would be easier than it would be for the wounded party if the break-upper were the first to move on. On the other hand, the new relationship would probably be quite painful for the wounded party to see.

Let's consider the wounded party—the person who did *not* make the choice to break up. There would no doubt be some internal conflict, don't you think? Yes, perhaps they would want to remain friends for the same reason as the break-upper—because they enjoy each other's company and still get along well. But they would also perhaps want to avoid giving up the emotional connection and what the relationship contributed to their life, such as laughter, confidence, and/or security.

Let's peel back the layers further. Our relationships help us to define who we are. We like routine and predictability, and when that's disrupted, we may have difficulty adjusting to the changes. We may begin to identify ourselves with the other person in our relationship, much as Tom probably did, so if our partner is no longer there in the manner we want, it might create an inner struggle for us. Will we find love again? Will we be as successful without this person? Who are we without this person? These emotional needs drive our Innatiousness. In short, we can't let go. Let's consider what happens when our Innatious intent is to get back together romantically with our ex.

INNATIOUSNESS WHEN SOMEONE HOPES FOR RECONCILIATION

Maddie and Lucas were together exclusively for more than five years. They hadn't gotten married nor had children, but Maddie was still very much in love with Lucas. She had ignored the signs that he was unhappy, so she felt utterly blindsided and devastated when he said he wanted to split up.

She talked it over with her friends, and given Maddie's narrative and perspective of the story, they suggested that perhaps Lucas was just going through something and needed some time.

With this undertone of validation from her friends, Maddie began to believe that Lucas did love her and would want to reconcile. Perhaps he was getting cold feet since he'd never been with someone as long as he'd been with her. So when Lucas agreed to remain friends with her, she jumped at the chance. He told her in no uncertain terms that the friendship didn't mean they'd be getting back together, and she told him she understood. But secretly, she believed their relationship could be rekindled if they continued to spend time together. If she worked hard to show Lucas what he was giving up, she was sure he would come back. In short, her Innatious intent in staying friends with Lucas was to reestablish their romantic connection because she was still in love with him.

But what about Lucas? Why did he agree to stay friends with Maddie? He was clear that he was no longer in love with her, but he did *like* her. After all, they'd been together for five years. He just didn't feel much passion for Maddie. He was hopeful that he'd be able to find a stronger passion for someone else, but he was also afraid he wouldn't. Maybe his relationship with Maddie was a good as it gets. So for Lucas, the Innatious intention for staying friends was to keep Maddie nearby in case his plans for a deeper relationship didn't work. In that way, she would be a fallback plan for him.

It was also true that Lucas loved the attention Maddie gave him. She went out of her way to show her love, and it fed his ego. It made him feel important, especially as he was stepping out into the unknown of dating once again.

All of this may seem selfish on Lucas' part, but he wasn't aware of these Innatious intentions. He convinced himself that he was staying friends with Maddie because they still liked each other and had a legitimate friendship. But underneath it, he had other Innatiousness that was less than charitable toward Maddie's feelings. If he had been able to uncover his true intentions, he might have thought better about putting Maddie in such a questionable position, possibly placing her at risk of being hurt again.

You can see from these examples that uncovering our Innatiousness is vital if we want to take good care of ourselves emotionally, as well as be empathetic and respectful of the other person involved. So we must be honest with ourselves about our Innatious intent when we contemplate whether or not to stay in friendship with an ex.

For Maddie, the situation was fraught with emotional peril. After staying friends with Lucas for more than six months following their breakup, he met someone else and severed all contact with Maddie. This time, the devastation was even worse for her.

While couples certainly do sometimes get back together, if that's your hope, please consider whether staying in contact could be damaging to you emotionally, as well as prevent you from establishing a healthy relationship with someone else. It's difficult to let go, especially if you'd truly like to be able to be friends. But if you're still holding a candle for your ex, you have to ask yourself if it's good for you to maintain that connection, at least in the short term.

Naturally, if you have children together as in the case of Carol and Tom, you'll no doubt have to be speak with and possibly see your ex at times. But remaining friends is something else entirely. That requires a bond between you that has nothing to do with the children.

OTHER TYPES OF INNATIOUSNESS WHEN STAYING FRIENDS WITH AN EX

Let's explore some other possible Innatious intentions when people wish to remain friends with an ex.

Jamal and Paula were together for eight years when Jamal decided to end the relationship. Paula had been very insecure throughout their relationship, frequently worried that Jamal would cheat on her. So she kept tabs on him all the time. If another woman tried to be friends with him, she got upset and made sure to stop it in whatever way she could. Even if he friended an attractive woman on social media who lived out of state, Paula felt threatened.

You see, Paula's father had cheated on her mother, so she was terrified she would go through the same pain that she watched her mom go through. She was determined she wouldn't let that happen to her, but in the process, she pushed Jamal away. Since he loved Paula, he stuck by her for eight years, but eventually, he just couldn't take it anymore.

Paula couldn't let go, however. She couldn't bear the thought of Jamal with another woman, so she told him she wanted them to remain friends after the breakup. Paula's *why*—her Innatious intent—was to continue to keep tabs on Jamal. She felt so out of control that she needed to continue to control him as much as she could. At least this way, she would be more likely to know when he got involved with someone else. If she knew, she would feel at least a little bit more in control ... or so she thought.

In the meantime, Jamal felt a great deal of guilt about the pain that the breakup had caused Paula. Even though he had every right to do what he needed for himself, he felt like a lousy person for doing anything that brought someone else pain. So he agreed to the friendship in order to hopefully make the transition easier on Paula. His hope was that she'd be able to let go gradually, and they would eventually break the ties entirely. Deep down, he wanted to be free of her and start a new life. His surface level thought was to be a good, loving person, but his Innatious intent was to avoid conflict. Those good intentions might not lead to the best decision for either of them, however.

As they entered into the friendship stage, Paula continued to question Jamal about his love life. She acted as though it was okay to talk about such things since they had become "just friends." But Jamal could tell that she was still trying to keep tabs on him, and it made him angry. He refused to tell Paula about any new love interests, so she resorted to asking his friends, who later told Jamal about her questions.

Staying friends only kept the couple tied to each other in an unhealthy way until Jamal felt the need to cut off contact with Paula entirely in order to protect his privacy and sanity. If Jamal had understood his Innatious intention for remaining friends, he may have realized that his surface level hope of being a good and loving guy was only a cover for his true Innatiousness of avoiding conflict. Deep inside, he knew Paula would likely struggle, but he didn't listen to his gut. He allowed himself to trust her words rather than pay attention to her jealous actions. He eventually had to concede that he took too much responsibility for Paula's feelings and needed to allow her to deal with her own issues of trust.

Paula would have benefited from understanding her Innatious intent as well. It's an unhealthy game we play when we believe we can control another person's feelings through manipulation. If she continued to avoid facing her fears and insecurities about being cheated on, she would perpetuate the pattern in any new intimate relationships.

These examples of Innatious intentions may make us feel uncomfortable. We don't want to think we have such intentions, but the truth is that they're human. Someone might even choose to stay friends with an ex because of financial dependency or unresolved sexual attraction. They might do it because they love the attention they get from their ex. Perhaps the ex still carries a torch, which makes us feel desired.

If we have these kinds of Innatious intentions, we aren't usually aware of them. In fact, if our underlying intentions feel unacceptable to us, we tend to hide them from ourselves. It takes courage to look inside and find such intentions that we don't want to think are true of us. It forces us to see ourselves in a way we might not like. But in doing so, we can learn to let those intentions go and have healthier relationships and a happier life. Paula's insecurities, for example, were wreaking a lot of havoc in her life. Coming to terms with them would pave the way toward freedom for her, as well as make it possible for her to establish a trusting and loving relationship with someone who truly wanted to be with her.

When we consider whether or not to stay friends with an ex, it's important to keep both our own Innatious intent and that of our ex in mind. Are we inadvertently keeping our ex from moving on?

If you're the one who didn't want to break up, it's important to sort out why you want to remain friends, or you may be setting up a bad situation in which you begin to feel used. It could be that a friendship will be possible after some time apart to heal from the breakup. As time eases the pain, our Innatiousness evolves, potentially making a healthy friendship more of a possibility.

Here's a question you can ask yourself to begin to uncover your Innatious intent in staying friends: If your ex asked you to get back together romantically, what would you do? Would you go back? If the answer is "yes," it's a big red flag that a friendship might not be healthy for you at this time. What would you feel if your ex didn't reciprocate the desire to remain friends? Would you feel hurt or angry? How would you feel if your ex entered into a new relationship with someone else? Would you be able to wish them well, or would you feel jealous and resentful? If you're still harboring jealousy and resentment, you probably need time apart. And sometimes, time is all that's needed.

So it might be best to give yourself the space to readjust and establish your new identity without your ex. Even if the decision to break up was mutual, it may be healthier to disconnect from each other for a while in order to fully separate emotionally and move on. Taking time apart allows you both to reestablish who you are without the other person in your daily life.

Of course, don't isolate during this period. Find support from friends and family, and distract yourself with activities you enjoy. Find new hobbies, if necessary. Over time, you will become more comfortable not having your ex around. You just have to get through the transition period.

You can also use the time to reflect on the relationship and learn from it. You may identify areas that you stifled or repressed within yourself in order to be in the relationship. As a result, you could find new freedom in being more authentically yourself so that you can bring all of who you are into your next relationship.

Allow yourself the opportunity to keep growing, and know that you don't need this other person in order to be happy. That can be difficult to believe, but it's true.

The bottom line is: If you want to have an authentic, healthy friendship with an ex, make sure each party has truly moved on and respects the other person's wishes and feelings.

EXAMINE YOUR REASONS FOR WANTING TO BE FRIENDS WITH YOUR EX

Let's say you broke up with your ex, but want to remain friends. What is your *why*? Identify the feeling you believe the friendship would give you. You may say, "I like them, and we have fun together," which may very well be true. But what is the *feeling*? See the list below to give you some ideas. Be honest with yourself, even if it's difficult!

1. To avoid feeling guilty.

2. To know you always have someone desiring you.

3. To have the security of being yourself with someone without judgment.

4. To avoid feeling like a "bad" person.

5. To avoid loneliness.

6. To avoid losing your mutual friends.

What if your ex broke up with you, but you want to remain friends? Then, what is *your* why?

1. To avoid being alone.

2. In the hope that they will want to rekindle the relationship.

3. To avoid the insecurity of the unknown.

4. To avoid losing your mutual friends.

5. To have the security of being yourself with someone without judgment.

6. To keep tabs on your ex's love life.

Once you determine your Innatious intent, don't judge yourself for it. Know that whatever it is, it's human. But if you feel that your underlying intention isn't healthy, it's up to you to take the next step and begin to heal what has caused you to have this Innatious intention. It's also up to you to stop the unhealthy behavior that comes out of that intention. For example, if you realize you want to stay friends with your ex in order to keep tabs on their love life, it's your job to be strong enough to say, "I think we need time apart before we can be friends." That way, you'll force yourself to face not knowing who your ex might be dating. You'll begin your healing process of letting go rather than holding on in a way that does you more harm than good, besides potentially ruining whatever future friendship might be possible between the two of you.

Whatever you find within, be gentle with yourself. Breaking up with someone is never easy, and it doesn't always bring out the best in us. We have many feelings that are often conflicting, and we have to navigate through them all in a heightened emotional state. Get professional help from a therapist or coach if you can, and strive to show both yourself and your ex as much kindness as you can muster.

9

Communication and Innatious

William and Erin were struggling in their marriage. It all started when William began to experience insecurity at work. He had a new boss who had different expectations than his previous boss. William found these expectations difficult to fulfill. He was suddenly supposed to manage many more direct reports, and he felt ill-equipped to keep up with so many people. As a result, he received a less than stellar performance review and began to worry that his job was in jeopardy.

The last thing he wanted to do, however, was worry his wife, Erin, about it. They had a mortgage, and Erin wanted to have children. William wanted kids, too, but he wanted to be more financially secure first. Since he didn't want to burden Erin with his problems at work, he clammed up whenever she asked him what was going on. Meanwhile, she couldn't figure out why he was so stressed. From her side of the situation, it just seemed that he was no longer connected to her and that he was keeping something important from her.

When she asked him if there was a problem at work, William just smiled and said, "Of course not." It bothered him to keep things from her, but once he lied, it became even more difficult to own up to the truth. Since William wouldn't share what he believed to be an embarrassing situation with her, Erin came up with all sorts of awful scenarios in her mind. Maybe he was having an affair. Maybe he didn't love her anymore. She responded by becoming prickly and irritable with William and snapping at him frequently.

William, in turn, began to think that Erin's behavior might mean she was no longer in love with *him*. She seemed to be annoyed by his very presence in the room.

After weeks of this behavior, the situation came to a boiling point. Erin snapped at William for leaving expired milk in the refrigerator, and he blew up at her for yelling at him over something so trivial. "Well, I'm not the one who's having an affair!" Erin shouted.

William was shocked. It had never dawned on him that his behavior would be construed in this way. Finally, he told Erin what was really happening at work. He explained that he wanted to protect her from worry and didn't want to disappoint her. But he had to admit that his Innatious intent was to protect himself from feeling that he wasn't good enough and that he was embarrassed. He couldn't bear to see the disappointment on her face, validating his insecurity.

William then wanted to know why Erin had been snapping at him so much.

"Because you've been so distant," she told him. "I understand now why you were acting that way, but since you said every-thing was okay at work, I assumed you were seeing someone else. I don't think less of you because you're struggling at work. You're human. It's okay."

Erin then thought about her own Innatious intent in being irritable with William. She realized that she was snapping at him to try to project some of her own pain onto him. When we make assumptions, we often think the worst as we are unconsciously seeking verification of our insecurities. For Erin, it wasn't so much retaliatory as protective, as her mother had cheated on her father. Unconsciously, she was trying to protect herself from further hurt.

"I'm sorry," William said. "I should have told you. I didn't mean to be distant, and I never imagined you would think I was having an affair. Now, I understand why you've been so irritable. I get that you were trying to protect yourself because you were triggered when I withheld from you what was going on with me."

When we fail to communicate honestly with each other, these kinds of misunderstandings are common. We're left to make assumptions, and those assumptions are often wrong because they come out of our most vulnerable and sensitive past experiences. This is why we're so triggered by incidents of dishonesty or withholding. Yes, these behaviors are built-in protection mechanisms, but our responses are impulsive and emotionally reactive. If William had cheated in the past, Erin's instinct to assume an infidelity might make sense. But since he'd never cheated, her response was an overreaction, just as William overreacted in withholding the truth because he feared Erin's disappointment.

There's a Chinese proverb that says, "Trouble comes from the mouth." Who among us hasn't experienced "trouble from the mouth" or miscommunication in a relationship? It's one of the main causes—if not *the* main cause—of breakups, failed friendships, and ruined business partnerships. Sure, there are many reasons for conflicts between people, but when we're able to communicate well, we give ourselves a much better chance of salvaging our relationships.

Obviously, we communicate with each other to convey information, but there are lots of reasons why our communication may be unclear. First of all, like William, we might be consciously hiding something that is painful to admit or which we fear will cause conflict. Second, we may be *unconsciously* hiding something both from ourselves and from the other party. This is when we don't know what we don't know (in business, this is called the "unconscious incompetent"). Other times, we sabotage ourselves, consciously and unconsciously, by allowing fears and old beliefs to cause us to behave in a way that isn't in our own best interest or the best interest of the relationship. Erin's Innatious intent would fall into this category. She didn't know why she was snapping at William until she stopped to ask herself questions about her behavior.

In yet another example, we might simply misunderstand each other because of the filters and schemas we use to interpret situations. Remember that schemas are the file cabinets in our brain that are like mental structures of preconceived ideas. We store all of our interpreted experiences and pull from them to make sense of any situation. Our schemas are the patterns through which we view the world, for better or worse. We can easily miss or dismiss information that doesn't fit with our schemas.

Erin was triggered because she associated the situation with a traumatic experience from her past, even though the current situation had nothing to do with her past experience.

This unconscious material is at the core of most communication breakdowns, and a big part of that unconscious material pertains to our Innatiousness. When we aren't aware of our Innatious intent, we might act in a way that doesn't serve us or the relationship. Plus, that lack of awareness robs us of the opportunity to communicate honestly with the other person. Innatious gives us a chance to be transparent with each other in a new way.

Imagine that both people are aware of what Innatious means and are willing to hear the other person's Innatious intent without judgment, like William and Erin were eventually able to do. Both understand that Innatious intent is always about fulfilling an unmet need and gratifying ourselves, but it doesn't mean we're selfish or lack caring for each other. That kind of honest communication can prevent the kinds of misunderstandings that plague so many relationships. Plus, when we see that our Innatious intent is dysfunctional, we can do the work to change it and give our relationships a better chance of surviving.

Remember, too, that how we rate our LAR scale has a lot to do with the quality of communication in our relationships.

We grow up communicating in similar ways as our parents because they're the ones who teach us to talk and relate to others. If someone has an insensitive way of communicating, we may adopt it without realizing it. And what one person thinks is insensitive is something another person might think is funny. Megan's friend, Claudia, grew up with parents who were lawyers, so it was customary for them to have heated "arguments" at the dinner table. They all enjoyed these argumentative debates and didn't let them get in the way of their relationships. Megan's family was the opposite. They were highly sensitive, so when there was a disagreement and an argument erupted, it became emotional and often turned personal. It felt as though the entire household might fall apart.

When Claudia started what she considered to be friendly debates with Megan, it caused Megan to feel attacked and stressed. When she would get emotional, Claudia was stunned. Luckily, Claudia had the self-awareness to explain to Megan that she was only acting the way she had been brought up in her family. Debating was a way of challenging each other for the better and conveyed an interest in each other's lives. In turn, Megan was able to explain to Claudia that arguments made her feel vulnerable. She told Claudia how debates in her home were more like earthquakes. With this knowledge, Claudia avoided starting deep discussions in an argumentative way, and Megan appreciated their thoughtful debates that weren't confrontational. Their friendship was not only spared, but thrived, with both having a greater understanding of themselves and each other.

Without that honest communication, Megan's LAR scale in her friendship with Claudia would have suffered. She didn't feel loved or accepted, and certainly not respected, in the face of an argument, no matter how friendly Claudia deemed it to be.

Since most of us communicate with someone else no less than 70% of the time we're awake, improving our skills is one of the most meaningful things we can do to improve the quality of our relationships.

THINK BEFORE YOU SPEAK ... OR LISTEN

Few of us think about the basics of good communication, especially in our closest relationships. We relax and assume all will be well, but that's exactly one of the reasons why those relationships often fall apart. It's like that old saying, "You always hurt the ones you love."

In order to avoid this, we need to be careful about what we say and how we say it. Before you speak, especially if it's a sensitive topic, consider:

- Why do you want to say this? What's your Innatious intent?

- Is your underlying intention to get revenge, hurt the other person, or manipulate them?

- Is what you're planning to say true, and is there a point that makes sense?

- How can you be more honest with yourself, as well as with the other person, and express what you really want to communicate?

- Are you careful of your tone and inflection, to make sure you don't rush to anger or accusation?

- What response do you hope to receive from the other person, and how will you react if you don't receive that response?

- If your Innatious intent isn't in the best interest of the relationship, do you have the strength to stop yourself from saying something damaging until you evaluate the situation more carefully?

Careful listening is equally important. Hearing is physical, but listening is mental and emotional. Most of us aren't great at listening because we've never been taught how to do it. Instead of truly taking in what the other person is saying, we tend to plan what we're going to say next, especially if we're trying to convince someone else of our point of view.

Part of the problem is that we think faster than anyone can speak, so our minds rush ahead and make assumptions. It's a survival/defense mechanism, trying to make sure we figure out quickly if we're safe (usually emotionally) with this other person. But when we rush in this way, we tend to rely on our filters and schemas rather than what the other person is actually communicating.

When listening to someone else, consider:

- What is your Innatious intent in this situation? Do you truly want to understand the other person, or do you have an agenda? Are you hoping to convince them away from their own point of view? If so, why? While there's nothing wrong with trying to convince someone of what you think is best, it's important to know why you want to convince them. It's important for the health of your relationship to then evaluate if your *why* is honest or likely to be hurtful. It's also imperative that you remain open to the other person's point of view and the possibility of adjusting yours.

- What would you like to hear from the other person, and how will you react if you hear something different? Are you able to receive an opposite opinion?

- Are you able to clear your mind so that you can listen to the other person with as few preconceived assumptions as possible?

- Are you prepared to ask questions without judgment to genuinely try to better understand the other person's meaning and intentions?

Interpretations become tricky because studies have shown that only 7% of what we receive in communication has to do with the words that are spoken. Voice inflections account for 38% of what we receive, while 55% is based on nonverbal behaviors, such as gestures, facial expressions, and body language.[2] While inflection and body language can give us information about the other person's true meaning, we can also easily misinterpret these signals. On the other hand, if we're open, honest, and transparent in our communications, our inflections and body language will have nothing to hide.

If you want to be a better active listener:

- Focus on the speaker, maintaining eye contact (without staring), and concentrating on every word, as well as the voice inflections and body language.

- Try to speak to each other in an atmosphere where there are no distractions.

- Nod occasionally to let the other person know you're listening.

---

2. Mehrabian, A. (1972). *Nonverbal Communication*. New Brunswick: Aldine Transaction.

- Don't interrupt. Let the other person finish before you speak.

- Try not to plan what you'll say when it's your turn because this will prevent you from listening intently.

- Periodically repeat or summarize some of what the other person said, and ask questions to make sure you've understood them correctly.

EMPATHY IN COMMUNICATION

As I have said, even though Innatious seems on the surface to be about our self-interest, it actually helps us become *more* empathetic toward others. Once we're aware of our human self-interest and how it isn't at all selfish but simply natural, our understanding of each other is more authentic and honest. We can recognize someone else's Innatious intent and empathize with their needs. This understanding also allows for the possibility of empathy in our *communication* with one another.

Sigmund Freud said that empathy doesn't require that we identify with the other person entirely, but that we identify with what they are experiencing. So as we understand someone's Innatious intent, we can put ourselves in their shoes and empathize with their needs and point of view. Of course, this is easier said than done.

We often get empathy confused with sympathy, but they're different. Both involve compassion for the other person, but sympathy is simply concern for the other person without sharing their feelings or point of view. Empathy is deeper than sympathy because we sincerely identify with and try to experience the other person's perspective and emotions. Both are appropriate depending on the situation. If someone has an illness or has just experienced the death of a person they love, sympathy may be most appropriate. It might also be most appropriate when we don't know the other person well. When our relationship is closer or we're experiencing conflict in the relationship, however, empathy can be the best way to establish deeper intimacy or understand the other person's point of view so that the conflict can be resolved.

Here's an example: Parent A and Parent B are friends, but it's difficult for Parent B to relate to Parent A's situation. Parent A has three kids under the age of ten. This person is a postal worker whose co-parent contributes very little toward child support. Parent B doesn't work outside the home and is a parent of two kids under the age of ten. This person receives both alimony and child support that covers the entire household monthly expenses with extra cash left. These are two very different situations, even though both people are single parents. Parent B could definitely sympathize with Parent A's situation, but empathy is going to require a bit more. Parent B must think about the emotional and financial stress of being the sole income-earner with little to no support from the co-parent. It's difficult and requires significant focus to put ourselves in the shoes of another person. But when we add an empathetic component, we enable ourselves to increase our emotional intelligence.

Of course, empathy comes more naturally to some of us than others. As human beings, we naturally try to avoid pain, whether our own or someone else's. Empathy requires that we put this natural tendency aside. Plus, if we feel anger or resentment toward someone else, it can be much harder to connect with our empathy toward them. But that's exactly when empathy is most valuable because identifying with another person, especially with their Innatious intent, can help us dissipate the anger and resentment we feel. It can help us understand why they behaved in whatever way that triggered our anger or resentment. This can then lead to the kind of communication that either saves relationships or at least allows us to part without lingering animosity.

When we listen to someone expressing their feelings, we can listen with empathy, but this often takes effort on our part. To listen with empathy, we must resolve not to judge the other person. We must listen with neutrality and try to understand their point of view. We don't rush to offer solutions to their problem. Instead, we just listen and let the other person know we're there for them, offering our support. We imagine ourselves in their situation. Empathy is a physical act, as we need to listen with both the mind and the heart in concert with one another. As a result, empathizing may feel emotionally draining, while sympathizing isn't. Yet, empathy allows us to connect more deeply with another person. This enhances our relationships, and sometimes, an expression of empathy alone is enough to resolve an argument.

Again, empathy includes withholding judgment even if someone handles a situation differently from the way we would. In that case, it may be harder to put ourselves in their shoes, but even when we can't fully understand someone's behavior, we can still empathize with their emotions and the Innatious intent behind that behavior. In other words, we can find empathy for their *why* even if we can't quite empathize with the *what* of their behavior. For example, Marcie made a mistake at work and was terrified of losing her job as a result. She lied to her boss about the mistake in order to cover it up. While you might understand her Innatious intent of wanting to keep her job because she's so afraid she won't be able to get another, you can't identify with lying. Still, you can have compassion for the *why* of her choice, even if you don't condone it.

Those of us who don't easily connect with our own emotions can find empathy more difficult. It's important to understand our own feelings in order to understand someone else's. We talked about emotional intelligence early in the book, so this is where that skill becomes a vital aspect of authentic and deep communication. This means that we can develop our capacity for empathy as we develop our emotional intelligence.

Once we finish listening to the other person's feelings and point of view, empathetic communication requires that we acknowledge their feelings and validate their perspective. Further elaboration is often unnecessary. We might simply say, "I understand why you feel that way" or "I understand why you did that." After you have validated the other person with empathy, they may wish for you to listen further. Your understanding may give them an opening to trust you and let you in more.

Validation may be difficult if the other person did something that hurt us. If they become aware of their Innatious intent and can communicate it to us, however, we may be more likely to find the empathy within us to understand.

If we're unable to empathize, however, it's easy to jump to accusing the other person. This frequently happens when we have no knowledge of Innatious. Then, we ascribe intentions to the other person's actions that may or may not be accurate.

Sometimes, we attempt to validate someone else's feelings, but we inadvertently *invalidate* them. A practical example is when someone they love is ill. We might rush to say, "He'll be fine." The implication is that the person shouldn't worry, but the reality is that they *are* worrying. While our intent is to comfort them, we're actually invalidating their feelings of worry. Validating their feelings might sound more like, "It sounds like you're really worried." Note that you don't assume the person is worried because you must acknowledge the possibility that you misunderstood them. Give them a chance to let you know if you're accurate. In this case, you reflect back that you've perceived they're worried. This is called "reflective listening."

Once they have confirmed that they are indeed worried, you might even add, "I understand. I would be worried, too" (if that's true). Then, if you truly have evidence that the ill person's odds of recovery are good, you might say something like: "I know someone who had this illness, and they had a successful recovery. So I have high hopes that will be the case here, too." The key is to first validate the person's *feelings* even if a part of us believes their feelings aren't justified.

Emotions are simply what they are. They're passing visitors that move through us, and they aren't always rational. If we can accept people even when our empathy is in short supply, we can often transform situations and help relationships heal.

As you strive to be more empathetic, guard against asking someone to think more positively. This is sometimes called "spiritual bypass," in which we rush to positive thinking before we've allowed ourselves to feel our feelings. This only serves to suppress our negative emotions.

Another caution is to avoid telling the person about someone else who has it even worse; therefore, they should count their blessings. While this may sound empathetic on the surface, we need to avoid the word "should," which invalidates what the person truly feels. If you catch yourself rushing to tell such a story, stop yourself. You might say, "I'm sorry. That isn't an appropriate story. Tell me more about what you're feeling."

It's also important to ask questions of the other person that don't elicit a simple "yes" or "no" response. Instead of asking, "Are you really worried?" you might ask, "Tell me what worries you the most."

EMPATHY IN ACTION

Daniel and Eva were in the middle of a big argument that was threatening their relationship. Daniel had lost his father at the age of ten. Ever since then, he felt a huge responsibility to take care of his mother and younger sister. He put it on himself to become "the man of the family." For this reason, he was very close to his immediate family. He spoke to his mother daily and to his sister every other day.

Eva, on the other hand, wasn't close to her immediate family at all. She felt she had little in common with her parents, two brothers, or sister. So she rarely spoke to them, and she hadn't visited them in more than a couple of years. As a result, it was difficult for Eva to understand Daniel's attachment to his mother and sister. She wanted to be the center of his life, as she had made him the center of hers.

The situation erupted into an argument when two weeks in a row, Daniel ran to his mother's aid at the last minute to fix a slow leak under her bathroom sink, leaving Eva at home to eat dinner alone. Eva believed that Daniel was treating his mother with more importance than her, his girlfriend, and she didn't understand why his mom couldn't just call a plumber. From Daniel's mother's point of view, he was the only person who had ever understood her old house's plumbing, and she didn't have the money to pay a professional. But for Eva, it made her question whether she should even think about marrying Daniel.

When Eva and Daniel finally sat down to have a discussion about this issue, they each explored their Innatious intent. Daniel explained to Eva that after the loss of his father, his family almost fell apart. He was only ten years old, so it was terrifying to think that he might lose his mother as well. He felt completely out of control at that tender age. In being there for his mother, he feels more in control and is able to quell the fear of losing control again like he felt after his father died. His Innatiousness is to feel less chaotic (in control), as well as to feel like someone who is needed and can take charge. His self-esteem was also tied to being what he considered a "good son."

Once Eva heard Daniel's Innatious intent, she felt more compassion and empathy toward him. She could put herself in the shoes of the little boy who was in such a precarious situation. In turn, Eva explained to Daniel that in her house, her parents put their relationship before the kids, which is usually healthy, but not to an extreme that means ignoring the children. Eva and her siblings were rarely told they were loved and were largely left to fend for themselves, which she came to realize was probably some neglect on the part of her parents. Then, in her first serious relationship in college, her boyfriend was very preoccupied with his career, not giving her the attention she felt she deserved. Their breakup was very painful for her. It validated the story she told herself that she wasn't important.

Eva's Innatious intent was to get Daniel to behave in ways that validated her as the *most* important person in his life. Upon thinking deeper, however, she realized she was actually jealous of his relationship with his mother. This was difficult for her to admit since she liked Daniel's mother a great deal.

But this is the power of digging deeper and using Innatious to discover our unconscious drivers. As Mr. Rogers once said, "If you can mention it, you can manage it." And as Maya Angelou said, "When we know better, we do better."

How would the LAR Scale help Daniel and Eva's relationship? Eva wanted to ensure that she got the love, acceptance, and respect she needed. She didn't want to repeat the same mistakes she'd made in the past.

When Daniel heard Eva's explanation of her Innatiousness, he felt more empathy toward her as well. "It sounds to me like you feel I've been neglecting you. Is that true?" Daniel asked Eva.

"Well, maybe, sometimes. When you run off at the last minute to take care of your mom, it feels like you're abandoning me. I worry that you'll never put me first. It feels like how my parents sometimes treated me."

"I understand that," Daniel replied.

As the two continued their discussion, Daniel was able to reassure Eva that he loved, accepted, and respected her. He agreed to be more thoughtful, to also include Eva when visiting his mom, and to ensure he didn't interrupt their plans to assist his mother unless it was truly an emergency. He would make an effort to create healthier boundaries with his mother, which he felt certain she would understand.

Eva, in turn, felt more certain of Daniel's love and respect for her. She was also able to put herself in his shoes, feeling his need to be there for his mom. As a result of this communication between them, she no longer felt as threatened by his attentions toward his mother and sister. Daniel, in turn, agreed to be more balanced about his need to always be the hero.

EMPATHY IN LIGHT OF CURRENT EVENTS

As I write this, the world has erupted in protests against excessive force on the part of police after the murder of George Floyd by a police officer in Minnesota. When it comes to the experience of racism, how can a white person empathize with someone who has been discriminated against for the color of their skin? As a woman and a lesbian, I might be able to find some common ground for empathy because I've been discriminated against as a result of my gender and my sexual orientation. Where does that put a white person, however, who might want to better empathize with the experience of a Black person?

It requires that we dig deep and truly try to put ourselves into another's shoes. There will be limits to our ability to imagine what it's like, however. We can't truly know another person's experience, especially when it's so different from our own. But we can use our imagination to help us conceive of how we would feel if we experienced the same thing. We can connect with any experiences of injustice that we've ever had and use that as a bridge to understanding. Again, we can't put ourselves fully in the shoes of someone who has experienced racism throughout their lives, and saying we can do so is offensive. But we can, for example, ask ourselves how we would feel if something like this happened to us or someone we love.

When trying to help others experience empathy in a situation like this, we might ask them to think how they would feel if such an injustice had happened to their own child. If someone murdered their child, wouldn't they go to any lengths to see the killer brought to justice, even if the killer were a police officer?

Remember: sympathy doesn't create change because it's more detached, but empathy provides us with the opportunity to change our point of view.

Whether we're empathizing with someone who is very much like us or very different from us, it requires that we be willing to step outside of ourselves to some degree and imagine what it's like to be someone else. Understanding Innatious helps us do this because it gives us more awareness of the authentic intentions of others, as well as ourselves.

EXPLORING YOUR CAPACITY FOR EMPATHY

1. Can you recall a time in your life when you grossly misinterpreted someone's meaning because of your own emotional filters? How did you find out that your interpretations were inaccurate? What was your Innatious intent in this situation? Write down your memories of this experience.

2. Can you recall a time when you were triggered by someone's behavior and overreacted to it? Do you know what experience from your past may have created this trigger/oversensitivity? What was your Innatious intent in this circumstance?

Do you think you can avoid falling prey to this trigger in the future? Write down your memories and feelings.

3. Have you ever inadvertently invalidated someone's feelings in an effort to help them feel better? Write down what you remember. Then, be sure to forgive yourself for not knowing better. How might you handle this situation differently after having read this chapter?

4. Is there a situation in your life now in which you could show someone more empathy? If so, how do you plan to empathize more fully?

10

It's All Up To You

Throughout this book, you've learned about the concept of Innatious and how it relates to virtually all aspects of your life.

In Chapter 1, you learned how our Innatious intent is based on an unmet need. Innatious can help us reach the top of Maslow's Hierarchy of Needs—Self-Actualization—and maintain that positive peak more consistently. You discovered how Innatious can help us become *more* empathetic, even as we seek to gratify our own needs, and you learned the importance of emotional intelligence to determine our Innatiousness.

Chapter 2 showed you how the LAR Scale can help you determine if your needs are being met in your relationships. It can also help you figure out true Innatious intent. Let's say you have a teenager who is upset because you won't let her stay out with her friends past 10 p.m. The first layer in this scenario is that she feels the need to be in control of her life. But if you apply the LAR Scale, you might see that her Innatious intent is to feel accepted by her friends. If she can't stay out as late as they can, she worries that they'll no longer accept her.

As you learned in Chapter 3, we teach others how to treat us. When we allow violations of our boundaries, we end up in victim mentality. What would be someone's Innatious intent for staying in victim mentality? There are a number of potential "whys," but often, it's because we don't want to take responsibility for what's happening to us. We don't want to consider why we allow someone to treat us poorly. So playing the victim might allow us to avoid the conflict of letting our true feelings known because we pretend we have no power in the situation, which allows us to continue to blame others. Either way, we stay stuck in an unhealthy situation.

In Chapter 4, you learned the reasons you choose the people in your life. You might find it helpful to apply Innatious to relationships from your past that ended, particularly those that ended with animosity. What was your Innatious intent in these relationships, and how might you have avoided the animosity if you had been aware of your Innatiousness at the time? Did you see the yellow flags of the person's behavior and ignore those indications? Why? Looking back to when you first got together, would you now have chosen the characteristics of that person? What do those characteristics mean to you, and how did having such a person in your life fulfill your desires and needs, even if they were unhealthy desires and needs?

Chapter 5 provided insight about our perceptions and defense mechanisms. Human beings are complex, so our relationships are also complex. But the more self-awareness and emotional intelligence we seek and obtain, the more capable we are of creating and sustaining healthy relationships. Up until now, self-awareness has stopped short of Innatious because we have traditionally denied that we want to gratify or fulfill our own needs in every life situation. With this tool for deeper self-awareness, we have a better chance of getting to the root of our fears and defense mechanisms so that we may see how we are protecting ourselves.

That's when we're capable of living authentically and transparently, as we discussed in Chapter 6. These are two key ways we not only reach self-actualization, but maintain it for longer periods of time. The less aware we are of the truth of our Innatious drivers, the more we feel we must hide. In that case, we operate from a place of tension, always needing to make sure the other people in our lives don't find out our secrets. Close your eyes for a moment and imagine a life in which you have nothing to hide. Feel how stress-free that would be. This is the gift of living authentically and transparently.

In Chapter 7, you explored Innatious in relation to assumptions, judgments, and biases. You learned about the concept of schemas and how they can keep us locked in inaccurate assumptions. Beyond our own personal assumptions and judgments, there are societal biases that have caused systemic racism and human rights violations around the world. Thinking about Innatiousness helps us unravel the "why" behind these prejudices so that we have a better chance of healing the psychological issues that cause us to treat others unfairly.

Chapter 8 was a very practical chapter about the possibility of staying friends with an ex after a romantic breakup. If we fail to consider our Innatiousness in these situations, we can cause ourselves or the other party unnecessary pain. It can be difficult to be honest with ourselves about the "why" of wanting to stay friends, but avoiding this always brings more pain than admitting the truth.

In Chapter 9, you learned about how to communicate your Innatiousness in order to be more authentic and transparent in relationships. You discovered ways to be a better communicator, as well as a better listener who listens with empathy. Communication is difficult and can be vulnerable at times. I give my clients who are couples a small communication exercise: ask the other person throughout the day what they're thinking. Each person is to state exactly what is on their mind, which could simply be thinking of going to the bathroom or grabbing an apple. Or it could be something more profound like feeling afraid their work presentation won't be good enough. The idea is to build trust by getting used to communicating what's on your mind.

Now, what will you do with this information in your life?

PEEL AWAY THE LAYERS

My advice as you explore Innatious in your life situations is to be sure to peel away the layers. For example, Pam and Ryan had been married for 19 years, but they lived apart during most of that time due to their careers. They didn't have any children. During the last five years of their marriage, they retired and lived together full-time. Although Ryan wasn't exactly abusive or nasty to her, Pam realized he wasn't particularly supportive. Ultimately, the two divorced, but Ryan was the one to initiate it.

Even though Pam was unhappy in the marriage, she was angry with Ryan for filing for divorce. She felt he should have wanted to work on their marriage. She had defined marriage as something you stick with for life. That didn't include divorce.

Nevertheless, two years after Ryan and Pam had split up, she had been able to find a new relationship. She and Ryan had stayed in touch, and one day, he asked her to take him to a doctor's appointment. She hesitated but agreed. She didn't tell her new boyfriend about it, however.

When asked why, Pam said it meant nothing and she didn't want to upset her boyfriend for no reason. But was that her true Innatious intent? When peeling back the layers, Pam had to concede that she didn't want to feel guilty, and she wanted to avoid potential conflict with her boyfriend. So her Innatiousness was a bit deeper than at first glance.

Then, there's Robert, who is an artist with a Ph.D. in art history. He's had a few opportunities to teach art and work in a studio to promote his work, but he didn't take advantage of them, claiming he was too busy. He said he really wanted to teach and work in a studio, though. "Since you want it so badly, how would it feel if you could do that?" I asked him.

"I would feel relevant," Robert said.

"Try to dig deep to determine what prevented you from taking advantage of doing what you want."

"I think it's procrastination and laziness," he answered.

When I asked Robert to go deeper still to determine his Innatious intent, he realized that fear of judgment/failure was his main issue. His need to avoid the fear of failure was stronger than his desire to feel relevant. Staying unaware of his Innatious driver to avoid these negative feelings could have prevented him from gaining the desired positive feeling of relevance. But he had to peel back the layers to discover his true Innatiousness.

Here's another example: Sports executive Wesley Branch Rickey made the landmark decision in 1947 to sign a Black man, Jackie Robinson, to play on his professional major league baseball team. When people asked him why he did this, he said it was good for the game, good for business, a sign of changing times, and a needed win for diversity. Although these were truthful answers, his true Innatious intent was embedded in a story from when he was a much younger man.

Rickey had been the manager/coach of a B-level team that had one Black player. Rickey saw this player suffer from terrible discrimination. While he told himself he did all he could to help the player, he later believed he hadn't done enough. We can speculate that he held that guilt for a number of years. While supporting Jackie Robinson was absolutely the right thing to do, his Innatious intent may very well have been to alleviate the guilt he felt from his earlier experience with the Black player.

What about Lori Loughlin and Felicity Huffman, the two successful actresses who engaged in the varsity blues scandal, in which parents paid to have their kids fraudulently accepted into top universities? In this situation, they both said they simply wanted the best for their children. Any parent can identify with that statement, but in this case, they broke laws. Plus, their children didn't know what their parents had done.

When we dig deeper about the parents' true Innatious intent, we might speculate that it was about prestige. Perhaps they worried that if their children didn't get into top schools, it would reflect poorly on them as parents. We may never know for sure, but it shows that the first answer about our Innatiousness is often not the definitive one. In other words, before you settle on your Innatious driver, take the time to dig deeper.

STRESS AND INNATIOUSNESS

When we don't strive to become more self-aware, we suffer much more stress in life. The more we understand our drivers and motivations, the more we can heal negative beliefs and fears. In turn, we become more authentic and transparent, and the less stress we feel.

This last exercise is to identify where your stress may be coming from in your life. When you know what areas are causing you stress, you'll know where you most need to explore your Innatiousness. This awareness will prevent you from jeopardizing your relationships by projecting any stress reactions onto others.

What are your current Life Stresses? *Rate each on a scale of 1 to 5, with 1 indicating little stress and 5 indicating significant stress:*

Family relationships

☐ **1**   ☐ **2**   ☐ **3**   ☐ **4**   ☐ **5**

Little Stress _____ *High Stress*

Friendships/social support

☐ **1**   ☐ **2**   ☐ **3**   ☐ **4**   ☐ **5**

Little Stress _____ *High Stress*

Job

☐ **1**   ☐ **2**   ☐ **3**   ☐ **4**   ☐ **5**

Little Stress _____ *High Stress*

School

☐ **1**   ☐ **2**   ☐ **3**   ☐ **4**   ☐ **5**

Little Stress _____ *High Stress*

Finances

☐ **1**   ☐ **2**   ☐ **3**   ☐ **4**   ☐ **5**

Little Stress _____ *High Stress*

Children

☐ **1**   ☐ **2**   ☐ **3**   ☐ **4**   ☐ **5**

Little Stress _____ *High Stress*

Health

☐ **1**   ☐ **2**   ☐ **3**   ☐ **4**   ☐ **5**

Little Stress _____ *High Stress*

Other

☐ **1**   ☐ **2**   ☐ **3**   ☐ **4**   ☐ **5**

Little Stress _____ *High Stress*

As you reflect on your scores, where will you look for your Innatious drivers that might be causing you stress? Are you allowing someone to treat you poorly? Are you living less than authentically or transparently? Do you have low scores on your LAR Scale in a relationship? Are you operating from a defense mechanism, assumption, judgment, or bias? Are automatic thoughts and negative beliefs standing in your way? Are you communicating and listening as well as you can in a difficult relationship? These are all important questions to ask as you explore your Innatiousness and work to reduce the stress in your life.

Final Thoughts

When I say it's up to us, I mean that we can't control others, but we *can* control our reactions and responses to what happens in our lives. In order to change those reactions and responses, we have to become aware of the needs that drive them—in other words, our Innatiousness. Unfortunately, sometimes, our need/Innatiousness is counter-productive. That's where the work of healing comes in that gives us the opportunity to create a happy life. Healing requires self-awareness, and that's why Innatious is such a vital tool for helping us improve the quality of our relationships with ourselves and others.

So when you're unhappy or when someone else displays what you think of as a "bad behavior"—whether a child, friend, parent, business associate, or lover—think about what their unmet need might be, and don't forget to consider the LAR Scale. Of course, don't assume you can know someone else's Innatious intent, but having the courage and tools—such as the ones provided in this book—to engage in conversations can help you build your compassion and empathy and create healthier relationships.

You won't be able to introduce the concept of Innatious to everyone in your life and have transparent communication with all of them, but I recommend you do so with the people who are open to it. Wherever you can bring it into a relationship as a means of communicating openly and transparently, you'll find the health of that relationship will increase exponentially.

Yes, the cat is out of the bag. It's natural and instinctual for us to want to gratify ourselves. The fact that human beings are driven to meet our own needs is nothing to lament. When we accept Innatious as simply part of our human makeup, we can see ourselves truthfully without judgment.

Integrating Innatious and then using it to build greater empathy is a key element to emotional intelligence and reaching that top level on Maslow's Hierarchy of Needs. Innatious is simply an important way to create a happier, more peaceful life for yourself and others in your life.

Acknowledgments

This book would not be possible if it weren't for two amazing women in my life. The first is my spouse, Scarlett Spring. This book has been in the making for over two years. Her consistent optimism as my biggest cheerleader gave me the confidence and courage that Innatious is needed in the world. Scarlett has also been my biggest advocate in implementing Innatious and truly understanding how it can lead to healthier and more fulfilling relationships. As we are 12 years strong in our relationship, Innatious has been a key factor in our communication.

The second amazing person I was so fortunate to find is Melanie Votaw. Melanie was the person who turned my dream into reality. Her professionalism, thoughtfulness, and skill have brought Innatious to the world. I am forever grateful to you both.

About the Author

Linda Buscemi, Ph.D. has spent more than 20 years helping a wide variety of clients to examine their behavior, build healthier relationships, decrease inner and outer turmoil, and create happier lives. She has developed behavior change programs for a variety of companies ranging from Fortune 100s to startups. A former radio show and podcast host, she is the cofounder of TapRoot Interventions & Solutions. Buscemi also coaches people on more effective ways to approach our most vulnerable populations, such as those with Alzheimer's Disease and dementia.

**For more information about Innatious, visit the
"Innatious" page on Facebook.**